GOLDEN TREASURES OF THE SAN JUAN

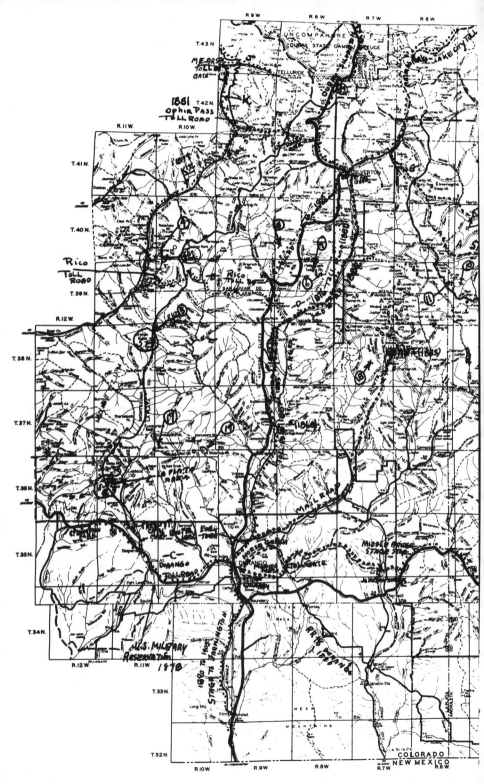

Map showing treasures in relation

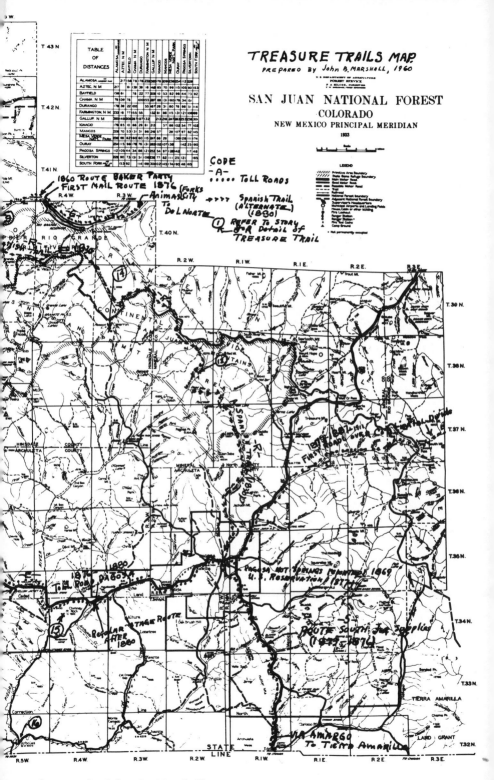

to modern roads. *John B. Marshall.*

GOLDEN TREASURES of the SAN JUAN

by

John B. Marshall

and

Temple H. Cornelius

SAGE BOOKS

SWALLOW PRESS

CHICAGO   ATHENS, OHIO   LONDON

ISBN 0-8040-0636-9
LIBRARY OF CONGRESS CARD CATALOG NUMBER 61-9435

Reprinted 1987

Sage/Swallow Press Books
are published by
Ohio University Press
Athens, Ohio 45701

To Treasure Seekers everywhere
who listen to the spirit of adventure

Table of Contents

Table of Illustrations

Foreword

To call attention to the nature of the San Juan region of Colorado a report of March 15, 1867, will be used. Lieutenant Colonel E. H. Bergman wrote concerning this region as a result of a trip made in January of that year. The letter was addressed to Major General J. H. Carletona:

"The severe inclemency of the weather and deep snows in the country east of the San Juan river were obstructions in my task.

"The extent of the country reconnoitered lies between the parallels of 36 degree 30 minutes and 37 degrees 49 minutes and between the meridians of 107 degrees 40 minutes and 106 degrees 40 minutes of longitude. The eastern part of area is bounded by the Sierra San Juan, its northern by a spur of the Sierra La Plata, the western part by the Las Animas river and the southern by Rio Chama. It's a wild country.

"The whole portion consists of a labyrinth of irregular mountains thickly covered with fine pine timber, some oak and good grass. On striking the trail up the Rio Piedra snow covered the area to the depth of two feet. Camp was established at the Hot Springs [Pagosa]. I and the guide started up the San Juan river and after wading through two feet of snow for about five miles, we came to the junction of the two branches of the Rio San Juan. At the hot springs several soundings were made to the depth of 41 feet and the temperature of the water shown to be at least 212 degrees [Fahrenheit].

"Leaving the San Juan river, we travelled in a westerly direction for some seventeen miles and arrived at Rio Piedra. A mountain chain is between the two forementioned rivers. From Rio Piedra to Rio Los Pinos is twenty-two miles over nine of which the trail leads through a very rough canon, walled in by lofty mountains. This canon impassable for wagons. Rio Los Pinos is from 70 to 80 feet wide and has a very rapid current with a fall line of 12 feet in a mile. From the head of this river to its junction

9

with San Juan river is 70 miles. The valley is enclosed on the northside by high San Juan mountains and on the west by rolling hills. While encamped here a snow storm of 40 hours duration was experienced. This made a heavy road to the Rio Florida a distance of 12 miles. Florida was a hard river to cross with a rapid current and being from 50 to 70 feet wide. Ascending the Rio Florida some five miles over extremely bad country the road turned at right angles toward the west and led through a ravine and over steep ridges to the Las Animas river. About fifteen miles up the Las Animas is a dense pine forest.

"In a level spot some two miles by three miles surrounded by high mountains on three sides and hundreds of miles from settlements we found signs of former presence of men. There were fragments of cooking utensils, agricultural implements, mining tools scattered among the fifty decaying cabins. A person not acquainted with the history of the area would have been puzzled by his discovery.

"In the latter part of 1860 gold discoveries were made in this area and Animas was founded by the Baker party. Perhaps many of the people were not of the working inclination and sought the gold without aid of manual labor. In addition on the third day of July 1861 the city was evacuated due to the war of the rebellion. However the unfavorable season and the deep snows in the mountains and limited time would not allow further exploration. Besides the natural obstacles there was the exhausted condition of my animals we planned our return.

"Some distance from the junction of the trail from the west and Rio San Juan, the trail became good running east through a gradually descending valley at the foot of 'Piedra Horada.' This is a peculiarly shaped mountain from 300 to 400 feet high running north and south for a distance of 15 miles. Along the summit of this mountain runs a perfect wall of plutonic rock and not much more than 6 feet wide and from 30 to 70 feet high.

"A short distance from Las Tapiaritas all observations became an impossibility, snow covered everything and it was extremely difficult to move the wagons. After a day's hard work the party arrived at Ojo de Hondo."

Bergman mentions the Indian tribes, and possible locations of forts to control their activities. He mentions that region will have a rush such as that of 1860-61 when settlers and prospectors are assured of protection from the Indians.

ACKNOWLEDGMENTS

To Sarah Platt Decker Chapter, N.S.D.A.R., p. 46-51 of *Pioneers of San Juan Country*, Vol. 111, Copyright 1952, Durango, Colorado, for permission to reproduce story of Rico Enterprise.

Walker Art Studios, Montrose, Colorado, for picture of Rico, and picture of Silverton.

State Historical Society of Colorado, Denver, Colorado, plates of early day smelter, near Silverton; of Rush to San Juan; of Crossing the divide. From the collection of W. H. Jackson.

Homer Reid, for photo of Ophir Pass.

Other plates from collection of authors.

To United States Forest Service for 1933 San Juan National Forest map, used as base map of endpaper.

The Lost Lone Wolf Mine

Skillfully concealed, by its original discoverer, in a brush-covered draw, somewhere on the western slope of Parrott mountain in southwestern Colorado, is a fabulously rich gold mine which has been the object of intermittent search for more than 60 years. There is no doubt about the existence of the mine or of its richness, but its exact location is still an unsolved mystery—a fascinating, intriguing puzzle, the successful solution of which would be rewarded by an incredible golden bounty.

The Lone Wolf mine was discovered as a sort of byproduct of the intense placer mining activity carried on by John Moss for the California Mining Company in the La Plata district in the 1870's. Moss founded the town of Parrott City in 1874 as a headquarters for his placer operations on the Bar—an extensive alluvial deposit at the mouth of the La Plata canyon where the river of that name emerges from the rugged mountains. The town was laid out at the southern base of the mountain on the west side of the canyon, and that peak immediately took its name from the camp.

In his preparation for hydraulic mining on an extensive scale, John Moss had ample financial backing from Parrott & Company of San Francisco. He hired lots of men and purchased a great deal of equipment in preparation for placer mining operations. It is said that Moss spent $100,000 cash on his undertaking; and that amount of money spent in any community in the late Seventies would make a lot of activity and bring the district wide fame. Parrott City became known far and wide as a new and booming mining camp.

Men from all over the West drifted into the new camp. Miners, prospectors, gamblers, adventurers, ore buyers, and just plain laborers came to Parrott City intent on making a quick fortune or in turning a fast dollar by fair means or foul, and then leaving for other climes. Parrott City became a lively, rough and tough frontier town. A good place for the man with some cash of his own, or a little stake in high-grade ore, to stay away from.

At this early date in the La Plata quadrangle nothing was known about the existence of rich fissure veins in the district. None of these veins had yet been discovered, and no hard rock mining had been done. Since Moss was preparing for placer mining, it was only logical that almost all of the early prospectors in the district confined their activities to hunting for placer gold along the streambeds. This circumstance left the rugged mountainsides practically undisturbed for the few hard-rock prospectors who were hunting for veins instead of placer dirt. And this condition made possible the secret discovery, the limited exploitation, and the subsequent losing of several rich mines in the area during this period. The Lone Wolf mine was one of them.

The late E. F. McCartney, early day freighter in the San Juan country, one time county commissioner of La Plata county, and in later years a mining man in the La Plata mountains, told the story of the Lone Wolf mine. Some of his information was from personal knowledge, and the balance he gleaned from old timers who were resident in the district at the time the events took place. (McCartney was never a resident of Parrott City. He came into the San Juan country sometime in the Eighties, but after Parrott City had "gone busted" because John Moss had failed to find pay dirt in the gravel deposits of the Bar.)

According to McCartney's narrative:

In the vanguard of the early comers to Parrott City while that camp was roaring with the first flush of its boom, was a lone wolf prospector—a deliberate and taciturn man who kept his own counsel and lived to himself. He was a young man, perhaps 25 years of age, but his rough clothing, faded cotton shirt, worn blue jeans, and heavy brogan shoes, together with his long whiskers and shaggy hair, gave him the appearance of middle age.

Lone Wolf did not tarry long in Parrot City itself. He bought a few supplies, asked a few questions about the mining activities in the district, and volunteered the information that he was a hard-rock miner who had recently worked in the mines at Leadville, and that he was interested in prospecting for veins, not for

14

placer. Then with his two burros loaded with his meager camp outfit, mining tools, and supplies, he left Parrott City to its own interests and traveled a couple of miles westerly around the base of Parrott mountain where he set his camp.

This was an area exactly to Lone Wolf's liking. The western slope of the mountain was not too steep or too rough, and it had an abundant covering of verdant vegetation, beautiful spruce timber, scrub oak brush, with hidden little valleys of lush grass for his burros, and plenty of good spring water. Since there were no major streambeds on this western slope there was no placer prospecting being done there and Lone Wolf had the whole territory to himself. He looked the whole situation over in a couple of days and approved it very highly. Then he started in to prospecting in dead earnest.

To him the western slope of Parrott mountain was an inviting challenge. Its serrated surface was covered with vegetation, grass, weeds, and brush, with very few outcroppings of the underlaying solid rock. To most hard rock prospectors this condition would have been a vice instead of a virtue; but not to Lone Wolf. He liked it. After he had spent a couple of days scouting over the mountainside studying the formations and sampling the few outcrops he found, he settled down to intense and careful prospecting in one particular brush-covered ravine.

Some where in this narrow ravine, down near the base of Parrott mountain, Lone Wolf encountered a small nub of rock protruding a few inches above the ground. He studied the lone outcrop for a few minutes before knocking off a sizeable chunk of it for closer examination. Then he got excited because the new break in the rock showed it to be a true fissure vein amazingly rich in gold. Lone Wolf had made his strike!

Just how much work Lone Wolf did on his claim is not definitely known. It seems certain that he drove at least a few feet of tunnel on the vein because he showed up in Parrott City sometime later with both of his burros loaded with rich ore which he converted into cash with an ore buyer there. Then he promptly got out of town without answering any questions. But he did not go back to his mine, not then.

Instead, he went to Alamosa, the railhead some two hundred

miles away, in the San Luis valley; and from there he sent samples of his ore together with a description of his property to H. A. W. Tabor, the mining man of the hour in Colorado at that time. Tabor had made millions in mining at Leadville and seemed to Lone Wolf to be a likely purchaser of his claim in the San Juan. Lone Wolf offered to take $25,000 cash for his property.

Tabor was favorably impressed by Lone Wolf's proposition and sent one of his mining engineers to inspect the property. The engineer had a check made out by Tabor himself in the amount of $25,000 payable to Lone Wolf if the engineer found the property to be as represented.

Lone Wolf met the engineer in Alamosa and together they made the long trip by horseback to Parrott City to inspect the claim. Examination of the mine satisfied the engineer of its worthiness, and back in Parrott City he proffered Tabor's check to Lone Wolf for the transfer of the property. Checks were not very common in those days, and Lone Wolf knew nothing about them. He had said cash and he meant cash—money, not a slip of paper. In vain the engineer explained that the check was convertible into money at any bank.

"You go and turn it into money then, and bring me the cash," said Lone Wolf.

"This check is made out to you," the engineer pointed out, "and you have to endorse it before I can do anything with it."

"What do you mean by endorse?"

"I mean sign your name on the back of it to show you are the one to get the money."

"I ain't signing anything until I get the money for my mine," retorted Lone Wolf. "You can't beat me out of my property that easy. I don't want to sell it anyway."

And with that statement Lone Wolf walked away—into oblivion for almost 50 years.

There was nothing left for the engineer to do but return to his headquarters in Denver and report to Tabor what had happened. So far as it is known this was the only attempt Tabor ever made to enter into mining in the San Juan Country.

Neither one of the characters in this drama realized the tremendous import that future events would give to their acts that day. Had the Lone Wolf prospector accepted Tabor's check for his mine, it might have been that Tabor would not have lost all of his fortune in the silver crash of 1892; and that Baby Doe Tabor, his widow, would not have kept her rendezvous with death in rags and abject poverty at the Matchless mine at Leadville; nor would the Lone Wolf have had to wander the lonely Nevada desert in privation and want while he ceaselessly prospected for another fortune.

The Lone Wolf's mine was gold and its value did not decline with the demonitization of silver in Cleveland's second administration in 1893. Tabor's mines in Leadville were silver ore whose value declined to the vanishing point during those distressing times.

In the spring of 1927 Robert McCartney and the late Milton DeLuche, son and son-in-law respectively of E. F. McCartney, were on their way to Mojave, Nevada, where a rich gold strike had recently been made. They stopped for breakfast in a small village on the edge of the desert. As they entered the roadside cafe they noticed a stooped, slender, and unkempt old man sitting on the bench in front of the establishment. They asked the proprietor who the old fellow was.

"Oh, he is an old desert rat common to these parts. He's been prospecting around here for a long time."

"Let's go talk to him," suggested Robert McCartney.

"It wouldn't do you any good," replied the proprietor, "he is a peculiar old cuss. Like most of these old desert rats he's got bats in his belfry. He is decidedly unsocial."

And "decidedly unsocial" was exactly the way young McCartney and DeLuche found the old fellow when they tried to engage him in conversation, until they suggested he join them in having a drink and breakfast. This kind treatment seemed to thaw the old man out and warm him up for conversation. When he learned that they were from southwestern Colorado, he remarked very matter-of-factly:

"I prospected in the La Plata mountains in that section nigh onto 50 years ago. I located a rich gold vein close to a town called Parrott City but a man by the name of Tabor and his engineer tried to beat me out of it, by gettin' me to sign a deed

17

afore givin me the money, so I covered the mine up and came away. I always been intendin' to go back and open it up agin but I hain't ever got around to hit." Then the old fellow shut up like a clam, and no amount of persuasion could elicit any further information from him, except that his childhood home had been "somewhar" east of the Mississippi, and in Colorado he had been called a Lone Wolf. Then Lone Wolf, for the second time in his life, abruptly walked away from his companions into oblivion—perhaps forever.

About 1908, McCartney said, the engineer that had represented Tabor in his dealings with the Lone Wolf came into the San Juan country again and visited the La Plata mountain district. He inquired if the big mine on the western slope of Parrott mountain was still operating. No one knew anything about it. The engineer then told the story about the mine and declared his intention of hunting for Lone Wolf's claim. But the country had changed from what it was on his previous visit over thirty years before. The oak brush had grown more in all the ravines, Parrott City had long since disappeared, and the few other landmarks he vaguely remembered as guideposts were changed beyond his recognition. His attempts to find the place were unsuccessful.

However, the engineer's story about Lone Wolf and the lost mine, and his efforts to rediscover the property himself, stimulated others to search for it. Among these was an old timer in the district by the name of George Brawner who had lived in Parrott City in the early day and remembered Lone Wolf. Brawner recalled a number of incidents in connection with Lone Wolf and the lost mine that confirmed the engineer's narrative; and these convinced Brawner of the existence of the mine.

Brawner was an old-time prospector, so he figured that with his experience, coupled with what information he had gathered about the location of the lost mine, he had a pretty good chance of rediscovering it. He fully appreciated the obstacles in the way of successful prospecting on the western slope of Parrott mountain. The absence of frequent outcroppings, the great amount of overburden in the form of earth, oak brush, and other vegetable growth, would make it extremely difficult to find any vein in that

18

region; but Lone Wolf had found one there, so Brawner decided
to make an effort to rediscover the lost bonanza.

Brawner spent a great deal of time, off and on, scouting over
the area and sampling all the rocky outcrops he could find. He
prospected along the crests of all the little ridges in the district on
the hypothesis that any vein in the area stood a good chance of
being exposed by erosion where it traversed the top of the ridge;
and on the same assumption he prospected the streambeds of the
open ravines in the area. But he avoided the ravines that were
filled with a dense covering of oak brush on the theory that so
much vegetation growth would prevent erosion from exposing
the underlying rock formation, and would cover any slight outcrop with an overburden of leafmold. In theory, this was sound
prospecting—but gold is where you find it.

Late one summer afternoon, after a long day of tramping over
the mountainside, Brawner stood at the head of a brush-choked
ravine. He was tired and hungry and was on his way back to his
camp at the foot of the mountain. Rather than climb to the top
of an adjacent ridge and follow that down to his camp, he decided
to make his way down through a patch of thick oak brush in the
bottom of the draw. It was when he was stooped over, the better
to work his way through this clump of brush, that he discovered
a loose fragment of rock protruding from the leafmold. To find
any sort of stone in this spot was something extraordinary, and
this fragment immediately aroused Brawner's curiosity.

He grabbed it up at once and began to examine it. Its irregular
shape and sharp edges told him it was not a piece of float or of
ordinary country rock. Its appearance, its very "feel," and the unusual circumstances under which he had found it, told him,
through that unexplainable sixth sense of a miner, that this rock
was ore. Brawner scrutinized the fragment, then he rubbed it
briskly on his overalls to get the surface dirt off, and looked at it
again. It looked mighty good. He was getting more excited all
the time. Then he spit on the rock and rubbed it harder on his
jumper sleeve, and looked again. This time there could be no
mistake. It was ore, and mighty rich! It was "plumb speckled
with gold."

Naturally Brawner was excited. Any normal man would have been under the same circumstances, but he did not let his excitement get the best of his good judgment. In his crouched position in the narrow, brush-choked ravine bottom, he looked all around him to locate, if possible, the source from which the fragment had come. He saw no outcrop anywhere, but a few feet away, right at the foot of the mountain slope, he did see a slight depression several feet long and filled with short, rotted poles and leafmold. He examined this unusual depression and found axe marks on some of the rotted poles, and in the course of stirring the leafmold around he found a couple more specimens of ore identical to the first one he had discovered. Brawner was convinced he had found the long lost Lone Wolf Mine! But since he had no tools with which to excavate the workings, and it was then getting late in the evening, he concluded he had better get on to his camp before dark and then make proper arrangements to develop his find.

Some time later Brawner told McCartney that he had found the Lone Wolf claim. He offered McCartney a half interest in the property on the condition that McCartney carry on the mining operations of the project, while he, Brawner, would look after the shop and the outside work. At the time McCartney was not in a position to accept the offer; so Brawner set about finding another partner.

He succeeded in interesting the late R. E. "Ross" McGirr, a member of the Otis-McGirr Mercantile Company in Durango, to the extent of accompanying Brawner for an inspection of the possibilities of the property. Brawner and McGirr took the Rio Grande Southern passenger train to Cima switch near the base of Parrott mountain and started up to the claim on foot. McGirr was in the lead. They had traveled a half mile or so up the side of the mountain when Brawner complained of being tired but said they were almost there and he could finish the climb before resting. A few minutes later McGirr heard a crash behind him and looking back he discovered that Brawner had fallen in the brush by the side of the trail, stricken with a fatal heart attack.

With Brawner's death active searching for the Lone Wolf mine came to an end. For a time following his demise different individuals made attempts to piece together the separate bits of information he had let slip about the location of the mine and to rediscover it, but as each new attempt failed and time again veiled the events about the claim in obscurity, the location of the Lone Wolf mine still remained an unsolved mystery.

The Lost Clubfoot Mine

Sometimes there is just no logical or rational way of explaining the reasons why some particular individual became a part of the rough and active life in a frontier mining camp. Clubfoot was one of such persons who came to the booming mining town of Parrott City in southwestern Colorado late in the 1870's.

Clubfoot was a stocky, middleaged man of ruddy complexion, fair hair, keen blue eyes, and a ready wit. He was a practical and prudent man, apparently normal in every way except for a congenitally deformed right foot. Hence his cognomen of Clubfoot. This appellation was voluntarily given him by the populace and he cheerfully accepted the title and offered no proper name in its stead. The designation was mutually satisfactory.

Clubfoot came to Parrott City well prepared for mountain prospecting. He had a string of three pack burros. Two of these were loaded with his camp outfit and mining tools, but the other one, a big, sandy colored jack, served as Clubfoot's mount.

"Hain't many men as can substitute four good feet for one bum one," remarked Clubfoot. "Sandy does my walking for me and together we git into some of the godawfulest places and git out agin. But without Sandy I'd be helpless."

Clubfoot was a "hard rock" man. He was not interested in placer ground at all.

"I ain't looking for gold in loose ground," he said when he was informed that most of the mining around Parrott City was for placer gold. "I want my gold in solid rock where the hole I make won't cave in on me; and I want the vein to be rich. I hain't interested in no other kind."

Clubfoot pitched his camp at the edge of town where water and grass were plentiful for his stock, and every day he spent astride the faithful Sandy in scouting around over the adjacent canyons and mountainsides in the forefront of the La Platas. Other prospectors in the same area who saw him or his burro's tracks in some of the roughest spots of the mountains readily verified the statement about "gettin' into the godawfulest places and gittin' out agin."

Clubfoot's method of prospecting on burro back was simple and efficient. Sandy's pace was slow and steady as he traveled over the mountain terrain with his human cargo. This gave the man ample time to watch for outcroppings and to study the formations. When he saw some ledge he wanted to examine more closely, he stopped his burro, dismounted, and hobbled, or crawled on all fours, to the place he wished to investigate. Meanwhile faithful Sandy stood on the spot where his master had left him and patiently waited for him to return.

"The man and the jackass make a good prospecting team," remarked a fellow who had observed the process, "the jack is the legs, and the man is the eyes, and they are both purty good."

Clubfoot did not stay around Parrott City very long. In his scouting around he had climbed to the top of Parrott mountain and had gotten a good look at the country beyond—particularly the rugged basin of what later became known as Root Gulch which lay immediately north and drained into the La Plata river. This area looked inviting to Clubfoot. In it he figured he had much better chances of finding veins of rich ore. And thither he decided to go.

In preparation for hard-rock mining in the back country, Clubfoot took his set of steel drills to the blacksmith shop to have them sharpened and tempered. The shop belonged to a big, powerfully built German who spoke English with a very pronounced Germanic brogue. We will call him by his frontier nickname "The Dutchman."

The Dutchman, a cheerful and friendly man, was reputed to be the best all-around blacksmith in the San Juan country. He was highly skilled in his profession and did his work with precise and meticulous care. The Dutchman fairly eminated friendliness, and he delighted in visiting with whoever chanced into his shop; yet he was discreet in his conversation. He never violated a confidence or let slip any information he had picked up that might cause friction or trouble to anyone. He typified that class of honest, rugged individuals who weathered the adversities of the frontier and helped to establish the permanent social order of civilized society as we have it today.

Clubfoot took a liking to the friendly Dutchman the first time he met him, the morning he took his drills to the shop. The Dutchman came out to help him unload them from the burro and he carried them in the shop and laid them on his forge.

"You vant the drill made sharp, yah?" asked the Dutchman.

"I sure do."

Clubfoot sat on the edge of the huge forge and pumped the old fashioned bellows to keep the fire hot while the Dutchman sharpened the bits of the drills. Work in the shop was not rushing that morning so the two men had time for conversation. They got pretty well acquainted.

Clubfoot told the Dutchman he was going back into the mountains to look for a vein, but he did not say exactly where he intended to go.

"Better you be careful. Other men into the rough parts they do not go. Alone you will be. To you something might happen. Bears there are. One might catch you," advised the Dutchman.

"Don't worry about me. So long as I got old Sandy I'll be all right," replied Clubfoot.

He told no one except the Dutchman where he was going. His stock reply to all questions was, "Too much civilization around here fer me. I'm fleein' into the mountains."

To get to his destination Clubfoot went around the eastern base of Parrott mountain and up the main La Plata canyon to the mouth of Root Gulch, and there he turned west and climbed a couple of miles up the rugged, heavily timbered mountainside to the upper basin of the gulch. There was no trail up Root Gulch at that time. Since most of the mining and prospecting in the district had been for placer along the main streambeds, few men had penetrated so deep into the higher mountain regions. Clubfoot, in his new location, had things pretty well to himself, and he liked it that way.

He pitched his camp under a big spruce tree on a grassy bench along the creek about the center of the basin and set about hunting for a rich vein. It is assumed that he found that vein very shortly after his arrival in the basin, and that, because of his deformity, it was located somewhere in the immediate vicinity of his camp. No one knows for certain, but other known facts make these conclusions inescapable. It is known that he found a mine and that it was a rich one, but just where it was located in relation to his camp has not yet been ascertained.

It was early in June when Clubfoot left Parrott City and went up into Root Gulch. No one saw or heard anything more about him again until near the middle of July when he came back to Parrott City to get supplies, and even then no one saw him until he arrived in town. In fact no one knew which way he had come until he told it himself.

"I snook into town the back way, and took everybody by surprise," he said. "I came 'round the west side of old Parrott."

The first place Clubfoot stopped with his string of burros was the Dutchman's blacksmith shop. Here he dismounted from old Sandy and hobbled around to unload one of his other jacks. The blacksmith recognized him immediately and left his other work in the shop to assist Clubfoot in the unloading process.

"Vare you been for so long?" inquired the big German.

"Over back of the mountain," replied Clubfoot with a nod of his head to indicate Parrott mountain. "Them's some drills I'd like for you to sharpen," he said as the Dutchman lifted a heavy canvas bundle from the burro's back and carried it into his shop.

Clubfoot got a small canvas sack out of his saddlebag on Sandy and followed the Dutchman into the shop.

"You do a lot of vork in tha rock since you vent from here," observed the Dutchman as he looked at the rounded corners and dulled bits of the drills.

"I sure have," replied Clubfoot. "I've driven nigh onto ten foot of tunnel since then."

"You find some gold, yah?"

"Take a look at this," and Clubfoot held out the small canvas sack. "But don't tell nobody nuthin' about it."

"I tell nobody noddings. When silent I am, it is smart I be."

But the Dutchman was not so silent when he poured some of the contents of the sack into his big hand and had a good look at it.

"Ach, Mein Gott em Himmel!" he ejaculated. "Dis ore, very rich

25

it be. The stamp of the eagle already it should have. Yah? You have more? Yah? You find the rich vein, yah?" In his excitement his questions fairly tumbled out.

"Yeah, I got more at the mine. I found a rich vein, sure enough. But remember, not a word to anyone about it."

"Nein, Nein, a word to no one do I speak," with a vigorous shake of his lionine head for added emphasis.

Briefly Clubfoot explained the situation to the Dutchman, but he shrewdly avoided letting slip any clue about the exact location of his mine or of any specific landmark that might be of use to anyone in discovering the portal to his tunnel.

He had found a small outcrop of a rich, gold vein, Clubfoot said, a few days after he had begun prospecting in Root Basin. The adjacent rock on the south side of this vein was not very hard, so that he was able to make good progress in driving a tunnel in the formation along the side of the lead. He had purposely made the opening of his tunnel small, so it would be easier to cover over, but a few feet underground he had dug the top or ceiling (called "the back" in modern mining parlance) much higher; and he had driven his drift at a steep incline in order to facilitate his getting the muck out. He said he mined the ore as fast as he got it "stripped" and allowed the waste material to accumulate in the mine—only removing enough of it to permit him access to the breast of the tunnel. That way he didn't have much muck to dispose of. He stored his ore inside his tunnel, and "throwed the muck in the creek, so's I don't have no dump to show where my tunnel is." He guessed he had enough ore stowed away "to load three or four jackasses." He always left his tools in the tunnel and carefully covered the portal when he was not in it.

He had run out of supplies, however, and had come to town to get "more powder, more candles, more grub, and my drills sharpened."

He hadn't come back via the La Plata canyon, the way he went in, because that way was "so rough and brushy"; instead, he had climbed up the mountainside to a pass in the divide, and had come around the west side of old Parrott. It was, he said, a much better way to travel. (The pass he referred to must have been the gap in the divide between the East Mancos and the La Plata, and which was later name Sunset Pass. There is a good trail through it now, but there was none in Clubfoot's time.)

Then Clubfoot made a proposition to the Dutchman. He had brought what he judged to be two pounds of his rich ore to pay for the stuff he needed and provide him with some cash, but he did not want to sell the ore himself because he didn't want anyone to know he had made a strike, and that would be sure to happen if he, himself, did the selling. But the Dutchman could sell the ore without involving Clubfoot in the deal and no one would be the wiser about the source of it. Now, if the Dutchman would do that, and would keep his mouth shut, Clubfoot would split the proceeds of the sale 50-50 with him.

The Dutchman "fersteid" and agreed. The deal net him $160 "vich was a goot day's vork," as he admitted when relating the experience in after years.

Clubfoot unobtrusively made his purchases and quietly slipped out of town, and returned to his mine. No one, except the Dutchman, had any intimation of his discovery, and The Dutchman, true to his promise, "kept his mouth shut."

How much work Clubfoot did on his mine after his return to it no one ever knew. He was seen alive only one more time, and that was about two weeks later when he made another trip to Parrott City. He did not bring his other burros with him on this occasion, but made a "flyin' trip" on the faithful Sandy. The blacksmith shop was closed that day because the Dutchman was away on business. Clubfoot, of course, did not get to see him. He confided in no one else, and after having made a few minor purchases, and posting a letter, set out on the return trip to his camp.

Exactly what happened to bring about his fatal accident was never fully figured out, and but for the action of the faithful Sandy, Clubfoot's death might never have been discovered. Late in the evening of the day following Clubfoot's visit to Parrott City, Sandy showed up at the edge of town. He was still saddled and bridled but the reins had been broken and the blanket was missing from under the saddle, otherwise Sandy appeared to be all right—no lacerations, no injuries, no bloodiness.

But to those who knew about the dependence of the man on the burro, and how reliable the jack had always been in his constant companionship with Clubfoot, the circumstances indicated that something unusual had taken place. The Dutchman was one of these. In fact he was quite deeply disturbed about the occurrence but he made no outward show of his inner concern.

The obvious way in which to solve the mystery was, of course, to backtrack old Sandy to some spot where information about Clubfoot would be found. But it was so late in the evening before any definite plan could be formulated and put into action that it was too dark to see Sandy's tracks, so the undertaking was postponed until next morning.

A group consisting of several horsemen from various walks of life assembled early in the morning to carry out the rescue mission. Among them was "a rough-necked old prospector called 'Sour Dough'" who was wise in the ways of burros in the mountains.

"It's goin' to be a tough job backtrackin' that jack through that thick oak brush," said one of the men.

"Hain't no job to it," retorted Sour Dough, "if 'en you know what yer doin'. Jest turn the jackass loose on his own sign at the foot o' the hill, and he'll foller his own tracks back to whar he come from better'n houn' dog could."

Accordingly it was done, Sandy was turned loose and started back up the mountainside, and true to that unerring instinct of a burro, he followed precisely the tracks he had made on his way down two days before.

High up the mountain, near the upper edge of the oak brush zone, the men found the missing saddle blanket and the ends of the broken reins at a spot where the knotted ends of the reins had become entangled on some gnarled oak roots and had, from all indications, held Sandy captive for several hours—until in his restless surging he had freed himself by breaking the reins in two.

"The ole jack was a bit restless," observed Sour Dough as he noted the torn up condition of the ground at that spot, "but, 'parently, he just kept a surgin' until he busted them bridle reins and got loose. He must 'a been skeered. We may find somethin' interestin' on ahead."

And something interesting they did find on ahead in Sunset Pass. There they found the lifeless body of Clubfoot where he had been fatally mauled by a bear. Exactly what had happened no one figured out. How Clubfoot got caught and Sandy escaped, or why the man was separated from his mount when he was attacked was never determined, and it is not of record that anyone tried very hard to solve the mystery. The tracks showed three bears were there—a grown one and two small cubs—and that the big bear had made the attack on the man.

The posse assumed that Clubfoot had encountered a she-bear with a couple of cubs and the mother bear had killed him to protect her young ones. And that verdict settled the matter. After all, the mystery of the missing Clubfoot had been solved, and it had been definitely ascertained that he had not met with foul play at human hands, so there was nothing further to do but close up his estate and bury the corpse. What did one dead man, more or less, amount to on the frontier anyway? Especially when that man had no close friends in the community. Clubfoot's pockets yielded nothing of importance, no paper, no letters or other information of his true identity, nothing but a twenty dollar gold piece, some odd small change, and a handful of nuggets—ore from his mine.

The party divided after finding Clubfoot's body in Sunet Pass. Sour Dough and two other adventurers of a similar caliber went back to Parrott City with the corpse, while the other two men followed Sandy on to Clubfoot's camp down in Root Gulch.

They found the camp under the big spruce tree on a grassy bench by the side of the creek, and the other two burros staked out nearby. However, they found no ore or mining tools at the camp, and nothing of a personal nature that gave any clue as to Clubfoot's real identity. After cutting a long blaze on the tree to mark the spot, the men loaded the meager camp outfit onto the burros and brought it back to Parrott City.

Clubfoot was buried in the crude frontier graveyard just outside town, his few effects were disposed of, the handful of rich ore was sold to a gold buyer and all the proceeds were put into a "kitty" and then his "estate" was assessed exactly that amount for "searchin' costs and burial expenses" and the whole party got on a big drunk with the money.

So far as the public generally was concerned, interest in Clubfoot ended when he was buried. One man, more or less, on the frontier didn't count for much anyway, and the only reason Clubfoot had been particularly noticed was because of his deformity. No one, except the Dutchman, knew about the rich vein he had discovered and worked, and that astute German was not doing any talking.

The absence of mining tools from Clubfoot's camp when the men found it was no surprise to the Dutchman. It confirmed what Clubfoot had told him about leaving his tools and his ore hidden in his tunnel. The Dutchman knew Clubfoot had a rich mine somewhere over the mountain in the vicinity of his camp, but he reasoned it was useless for him to try to find it. He was neither miner nor mountaineer himself, and would have no idea how to proceed in the search; and he knew of no one he could trust to share the undertaking with him, so he did nothing about it.

The handful of nuggets found in Clubfoot's pocket, however, aroused considerable curiosity and speculation. Everyone figured he had gotten them from a rich vein somewhere in Root Gulch. Old Sour Dough expressed his convictions after he had taken a few drinks paid for by "the expense funds from the estate":

"That old boy had somethun' purty rich over thar somewhar and I aim to go over and find it."

But old Sour Dough never had an opportunity to carry out his plan. The old renegade got into trouble while he was drunk that evening and had to skip out of the country to save his neck.

Several other men had the same idea but a rainy spell prevented any of them from undertaking the hunt immediately, and by the time the first of them did get over into Root Basin, the rains had obliterated all fresh signs of any activities Clubfoot had carried on, and had made whatever covering he had put over the portal of his tunnel appear as a natural part of the ground around it. They found his campsite but no one found the mine.

Several years later, sometime in the early Eighties, after the Denver and Rio Grande railroad had been built into the new town of Durango, a man came into the city on other business. In the meantime placer mining at Parrott City had proved a failure, and that camp had been abandoned and its inhabitants had moved away.

The visitor inquired about Parrott City, and when informed that the place was only a ghost town, he said a granduncle of his had found a rich vein somewhere in the vicinity of that town several years previous. The granduncle, a clubfooted man, had written his sister (the visitor's grandmother) about his mine, and had expected to market enough ore to give him a substantial stake that fall; but the granduncle had never been heard from after that time. Since he was a sort of wandering globe trotter anyway who seldom wrote letters home, the folks assumed that the rich strike had not proved out so good, and that the uncle had moved on to other climes as was his wont without ever taking the trouble to let the home folks know about it.

The visitor said he had never known his clubfooted granduncle, had no great interest in the matter, and all the knowledge he had about the mine was that which he had gathered from conversations he had heard among his relatives.

He tried during the limited time of his stay in Durango to contact some former resident of Parrott City who knew a clubfooted man there, but without success. Several weeks after he had departed, the Dutchman heard his story and then, for the first time, the Dutchman gave his version of what had happened.

And the legend of the lost Clubfoot mine was definitely established.

These stories renewed men's interest in the lost bonanza, and the discovery of the fabulous Comstock mine, a rich producer, at the mouth of Root Gulch a couple of miles down the mountain from Clubfoot's camp, gave added impetus to the search which gradually subsided as mining in the immediate area became less active. Then, just after the turn of the century, the Lucky Moon vein was discovered in a side canyon of Root Gulch, south of Clubfoot's old camp, and interest in the lost mine was revived. At about the same period of history the Mountain Lily, another mine of bonanza quality, was opened a mile or so north of Clubfoot's old camp and produced a fortune in gold before it was worked out. Then in the 1930's, the Red Arrow Mine, the most fabulous and the most spectacular of them all, was discovered on the East Mancos canyon at a spot directly west, through the divide, from Clubfoot's location. Ore on the Red Arrow was so rich that gold nuggets as large as a hen's egg were not uncommon, and they were of such purity that they were shipped directly to the United States mint in Denver—a most extraordinary occurrence in mining activities.

While none of these rich mines was the lost Clubfoot workings, they were all located in that immediate area and were tangible proof that it was a richly mineralized district. The possibility that the amazing Red Arrow, because of its location on the western slope of the same ridge, could be the western terminus of Clubfoot's lost vein has been pointed out by many different mining men.

It has been discovered that strange geological things happen to rich veins in the La Platas.

The lost Clubfoot mine has not yet been found, but some day some lucky person, scouting around in the vicinity of his old camp in Root basin, will find an outcrop of his rich vein, or will discover where the forces of nature have exposed, by wind and storm, some of the telltale coverings he put over the portal of his rich treasure tunnel, and in doing so will open the door to a golden fortune. And that someone will not necessarily be a miner or a prospector. He may be a hunter, a tourist, or a hiker. He may be you. As for me, I am going to take a hike in Root basin this summer.

Milt Hollingsworth's Venison Lode

Deer hunting and prospecting are two very divergent occupations, but there are times when a man can do both jobs and find a rich vein while he is doing it. That is what Milt Hollingsworth did high up on the side of Parrott Mountain in southwestern Colorado about the turn of the century.

Hollingsworth was an old timer in the La Plata country. He was one of the pioneers who came to Parrott City when that bustling mining camp was first established, and had followed mining and prospecting as a major occupation since that time. When the placer mining boom around Parrott City failed because there was not enough placer gold in the gravel to make it pay, Hollingsworth turned his attention to hard-rock mining which then was just beginning to come into its own in the district. He built himself a nice cabin a little way up the La Plata canyon and in the center of a rich mining area.

He made his living by working as a miner in the producing mines of the district. He worked on the Comstock, a rich bonanza of the La Platas in an early day; on the Southern Boy, the old Cumberland, and other mines of that period. He gained a lot of knowledge of mineralogy, geological formations, and characteristics of the various ores of the district while working on these properties. He did assessment work for other men on their claims, and took some good, commercial ore out of his own properties. He prospered and did well. His practical knowledge of mining enabled him to make some very rich discoveries for other people while working on their claims.

Hollingsworth always found time to hunt and prospect over the adjacent canyons and mountainsides. It was said of him that he was as familiar with the broken terrain in that district as a child was with his playground. Always on these combined hunting-prospecting trips he took samples of any ledges and veins that he thought might contain values in metals. He would test

33

these samples later himself or send them to an assayer for analysis. If the assays showed sufficient values in any of the samples to justify investigation of the vein, he always remembered the place where he had taken that sample, and never had any difficulty in returning to the exact spot. He found several valuable claims in this way.

He was out hunting late in October, 1901; the weather was cloudy and threatening storm. Hollingsworth was in a hurry to get his venison before snow came in the high country to make hunting more difficult. He had found fresh deer tracks high up on the mountainside west of his cabin and was following them along a dim game trail through the forest when he noticed the outcropping of a vein, on the steep point of ridge between Root Gulch and Snowslide Draw.

Obeying his miner's impulse, he immediately stopped to investigate it. He broke off a good-sized specimen from the protruding nub of rock and looked at it carefully. He immediately recognized it as sylvanite, an ore of the telluride group, which carried considerable value in gold. He did not investigate further at the time, however, because there would be ample time to do that later after he got his venison. The vein, he knew, would remain where it was. It would not run away, but not so with the deer. It had legs and could move about; and he had better follow the deer's tracks while they were fresh. He hastened to put the sample of ore in his hunting sack and to take careful note of the location. From this spot he could see several familiar landmarks, among which were the buildings at the Southern Boy mine on the opposite side of the La Plata canyon, an open spot on the floor of the canyon just below his own cabin, the Gold King dump over on the side of Lewis mountain, and on open patch of rimrock below him and on the opposite side of Snowslide Draw. Having thus set the location of the outcrop firmly in mind, Hollingsworth went on about the important business of getting some fresh venison to replenish his larder. He got his deer all right, about a half mile farther on in the edge of the timber at the head of Snowslide Draw. He hung the carcass to a spruce limb with a piece of wire he had with him, and after he finished dressing it, he cut the hind feet off and left them hanging from the bough and took the meat home with him. And just in good time, too, because that evening it began to snow.

With a slight covering of snow on the ground, Hollingsworth made no attempt to return to his new find immediately. He was not overly anxious about it, anyway. He had made many discoveries of ore before, much in the same manner, and had deferred investigating them until some convenient later date. He would do the same with this one. The finding of ore was no new experience to Hollingsworth.

Hollingsworth examined his sample more carefully after he got to his cabin that evening. He was convinced that it was by far the richest find he had ever made. To avoid any possibility of getting it mixed up with any of his other samples, he put it back in his hunting bag and hung the bag up on the wall in its usual place. This was the only specimen of rock he had picked up that day.

For the following few days Hollingsworth busied himself about finishing up a few odd jobs he wanted to get done before the heavy snows of the winter came. In the meantime the snow storm continued intermittently until the mountains were covered with a deep blanket of it, which, of course, would put an effective end to prospecting and all other outside work until the following spring.

Hollingsworth took advantage of this lax time to test, for their richness, whatever samples he had on hand. The first one he tested was the one he had in his hunting bag—the one he had gotten while hunting the deer. He was almost dumfounded with the results of his simple analysis. He could hardly believe them. The ore was far richer than he had expected it to be. It was of bonanza quality! To check on the accuracy of his own work, he sent some of the ore to an assayer for a more careful analysis. The returns from this source were even more startling than his own. That ore was worth $40,000 per ton! (And that was at the old price of gold. It would be 75% more now, or $70,000.)

Realization of the magnitude of his discovery gave Hollingsworth that incomparable thrill, that undefinable inner exultation that only a mining man can really understand—an inner happiness

35

and contentment of spirit that has no parallel in any other line of human endeavor.

But with all of his exultation Hollingsworth was discreet. He carefully kept his mouth shut and told no one about his discovery. Such information would have caused a stampede of prospectors into the area early in the spring. Silence was the better part of wisdom in this instance, and Hollingsworth was a wise man in mining matters.

Impatiently he waited for spring to come when he could go back up the mountain, find the outcropping again, stake it, and begin to take out his fortune. With ore of such high quality, right on the surface, a big fortune could be taken out in a short time and with a minimum expenditure of time and money. Such an opportunity comes to few men in a lifetime. It had never come to Hollingsworth before, and he intended to take full advantage of it now.

Long before the snow had melted off the mountain slopes the following spring, Hollingsworth was making prospecting trips over that hillside. Impatiently he watched the slowly receding snow line, confidently expecting to rediscover his coveted vein just as soon as the snow melted off it.

But the snow melted away completely, and yet he did not find the elusive outcrop. Day after day he climbed the mountain and diligently searched over the area without success. He knew he was in the vicinity of it, he knew this was the place where he had stumbled onto the vein the past autumn. He could see the various landmarks he had so carefully noted at that time, but to his chagrin he discovered that he could see these landmarks from innumerable points in this area. He could not use them as guide-posts to the exact spot. He followed around the mountainside into the head of Snowslide Draw where he had dressed the deer the day he found the vein, and he found the hind shanks still hanging from the limb as he had left them on that occasion, but this did not help him to find the precise spot where the rich ledge broke the surface of the ground. He held firmly in his mind the picture of how the spot looked after he had broken the sample off from the vein—no other outcrop on the whole hillside would look the same as it did. When he broke off the protruding nub of the outcrop the preceding autumn the break had left a scallop or a sort of half moon shape in the ledge with a rather slender and sharp protruding horn on the lower side. This, he knew, would be an unmistakable identifying mark of the vein, but he could find no rocky outcrop of any sort with a scallop of that shape. It was just simply not to be found; yet Hollingsworth knew he had found it there the previous fall. And he knew this area was in gold country—the fabulous Comstock at the mouth of Root Gulch was not far away, and the rich, lost Clubfoot mine in upper Root basin was even closer, but these facts only exasperated him more. They did not help to find his vein.

For two successive summers Hollingsworth bore his disappointment and conducted his solitary search in silence, always hoping that each trip would prove successful. He could not figure out why he could not find the rich outcrop again. He couldn't understand what had happened to it. The third summer he confided in a fellow miner, relating to him all the circumstances, and inviting him to join in the search.

Together they searched for the lost bonanza on all of their week ends and "off days" during the whole season. They found some pieces of float—loose pieces of ore detached from the main vein and eroded away from it—of the same character, quality, and value as Hollingsworth had broken from the original outcrop, but they never found the solid vein in place as he had done.

Then, about 1905, the amazing Lucky Moon vein was discovered, through a freakish coincidence, in a side draw of Root Gulch about a quarter mile north and a little west from the point of mountain where Hollingsworth had made his fabulous find, but the Lucky Moon was not the Hollingsworth.

Hollingsworth himself visited the Lucky Moon after its discovery and said it positively could not be the lode he had found four years before. On that memorable occasion he had crossed a little flat about three hundred yards below the Lucky Moon, he said, and had gone through the timber around the mountainside southward to the point of mountain, and there he had made his discovery.

The ore on the Lucky Moon was of a similar character to that of Hollingsworth's vein, but it was not the same nor was it so

37

rich. It was more of a tellurium while the other was a true sylvanite. However, both ores are of the telluride group.

The Lucky Moon was to be a rich producer, but its vein system proved to be erratic "stringers"—offshoots—from some main vein located somewhere in the adjacent geological formation. Experienced mining men in the region believe that the outcrop that Hollingsworth found is that main vein or "mother lode to the Lucky Moon." Considering the rich production of the Lucky Moon, if that mine was only a descendent, the riches of the mother lode would stagger a man's imagination.

What happened to Hollingsworth's outcrop that he could never find it again? He hunted for it intermittently up to the time of his death a good many years ago. The vein, of course, is still there. It did not evaporate, disseminate, or transmute into something else or recede back deep into the ground; nor has some occult, sinister, superhuman force come along to conceal it in some supernatural manner. Whatever happened to cover it over was a natural occurrence which might be so simple and so obvious as to escape observation. The annals of mining in the mountainous country of the West contain many similar incidents. The fresh break Hollingsworth made in the outcrop when he took his sample would, of course, not remain fresh and bright very long. In the course of a few weeks that exposed surface would become dulled through oxidation and exposure to the weather. The shape of the "break" was such as to catch and to hold dirt and leafmold thrown onto it by wind and storm. Experienced miners and prospectors of the region believe that is exactly what has happened; similarly, they reason that as the forces of nature have covered it over, those same forces will also uncover it again. Very possibly these forces uncovered it many times, but no one has come along to observe it at the right time.

Time has dulled the interest in Hollingsworth's ledge. Many of the old-timers who knew about it have passed on and newcomers have taken their places, but to this day men still hunt for this rich, lost vein; they still find bits of "float" in the area—indisputable evidence of the existence of a rich vein nearby—but as yet no one has been fortunate enough to open this concealed door to uncounted millions. Possibly only a half inch of leafmold is the inscrutable curtain that hides that golden portal. A hard summer shower can easily remove that curtain in a few moments and expose that outcrop more plainly than it was when Hollingsworth found it. Fortunate, indeed, will be the man who passes that way then and is observant enough to note that open invitation to golden wealth.

Rico, the Enterprise Mine, and a Short Straw

Rico—rich—what a world of romance and adventure that name connotes! And that fabulous little mining camp located deep in the Rockies on the head of the East Dolores River, for the few short years of its heyday, fulfilled all the connotations expected from it. Fabulous riches, and stark poverty; fame and fortune for some, failure and oblivion for others; lucky breaks for some and adversity for others: these were all a part of life in Rico, where momentous decisions were made by trivial incidents and the location of a multi-million dollar shaft was determined by the drawing of the shortest straw. And a long chance on the lucky ticket in a Louisiana Lottery helped to finance the shaft that discovered the fantastic Rico blanket vein that produced millions in treasure, and made possible the most extensive underground workings in all of Colorado up to the turn of the century.

In all this maze of heterogeneous activities the name of one man stands out prominently, and the goddess of good luck beneficiently favored him in several crucial instances. That man was Dave Swickheimer.

The Rico area was originally a part of the Ute Indian territory in which white men had no legal right to intrude, but despite this prohibition, a number of intrepid adventurers went into the region in the late 1860's. Among these were Joe Fearheiler and Sheldon Shafter, who located the first mining claim, the Pioneer, in 1869, and who built the first cabin in the area, a log structure on Silver Creek. These men were followed by others in rapid succession, and there was considerable clamor for the district to be opened legally for mining and prospecting.

In response to this popular demand the federal government concluded the Brunot Treaty with the Ute tribe in 1873 and thereby threw this area of the Rocky Mountains open to mining and prospecting. Dave Swickheimer came to Rico with the influx of population that followed—a colorful character in a colorful background.

In Rico, as in all new mining camps on the raw and unorganized frontier, excitement, hope, and the selfish zest of the battle for possession of mining claims dominated all activities. Life was turbulent, and competition was keen. The Rico district was new and unexplored, its vein system and its geological formations were as yet unknown. This condition, however, made little difference to the majority of prospectors who came into the region because they were ignorant of the basic principles of mining and of geology. Many of them did not know that ore came in veins, and that veins occur under certain conditions. Instead of looking for surface indications of a vein before beginning to dig a shaft, many of them began to dig anywhere that suited their fancy, working on the assumption that ore would ultimately be encountered in their diggings. Existence of the great Rico Blanket vein, that stupendous geological freak, that later made the Enterprise mine such a rich producer, was as yet unknown.

The early strikes of rich lead carbonate ore, first on the Pioneer in 1869, and later by the Robert Darling party in 1872, on the first outcropping which was located on the north end of what later became the main street of Rico, stimulated the influx of population into the district. The real stampede of miners and adventurers, however, began in 1878 and increased in 1879.

In 1878 John Glasgow, Charles Hummiston, and Sandy Campbell located the Atlantic Cable, Grand View, Phoenix, and Yellow Jacket claims, and in 1879 they sold the Grand View to Jones and Mackay of Virginia City fame, for the magnificent sum of $100,000. Then to add to this stimulating excitement, Colonel J. C. Haggarty early in 1879 sent some samples of ore from his claim on Nigger Baby Hill to Ouray to be assayed. The samples proved to be lead carbonate, extremely rich in silver. News of this strike and of the sale of the Grand View caused a stampede of miners from Ouray, Silverton, and other districts into the Rico area and the mining boom was on! The "Second Carbonate" had been discovered! In the mad scramble to locate claims anywhere in the vicinity of the strikes, all available ground was staked and cross-staked regardless of whether or not there was a mineral bearing vein in sight on the claim, although the presence of such a ledge was a legal requirement in order for the claimant to hold his property against an adjoining claimant who did have a vein in sight.

Dave Swickheimer was in this rush and rode the vicissitudes of fortune up and down until the bounty of Lady Luck showered him with magnificent riches.

Let us trace the delicate silver thread as Lady Luck weaves the intricate design on the fabulous pattern of circumstances that ultimately made this persistent miner a millionaire.

In the spring of 1881, Swickheimer and his two partners, Patrick Cain and John Gault, decided to sink a shaft on their mining claim, the Enterprise, located on top of Enterprise Hill, a flat-topped promontory in the active mining area of Rico. Since there was no vein or outcrop of ore showing on the surface of their claim, location of the shaft was a rather random affair. Apparently, one spot was as good as any other in which to sink the shaft in quest of ore. One partner favored a location near the east line of the claim, another selected a spot farther north, while the third one chose a place several feet inside from the east boundary, because it looked like an easy spot to begin digging. Good naturedly the partners agreed to draw straws in order to decide the matter. The man drawing the shortest straw should select the site. Lady Luck gave the shortest straw to the man who selected the "easy spot to begin digging," well inside the east boundary, and that was where the shaft was put. The digging was not so easy, however, after the first few feet of loose earth were removed and the solid rock underneath had to be drilled by hand and the muck hoisted to the surface with an old fashioned hand windlass, known among miners as a "bean hoist." The project was abandoned at a depth of 35 feet, and the three owners sold their claim to George Barlow, who sank a shaft to a depth of 146 feet on the adjoining claim, the Songbird, without encountering any ore. In 1883 the Enterprise shaft was discredited and abandoned.

In the meantime Swickheimer had been working in the Swansea mine, which had a true fissure vein and was located down the mountainside from the Enterprise. Through the knowledge that he gained from observation and experience while on the Swansea, Swickheimer was convinced that the Swansea vein extended into the Enterprise, but by this time that claim had been relocated by Barlow and Waggoner; so in order to regain an interest in the property, Swickheimer had to buy Waggoner out. This deal took about all the capital Swickheimer had. Very little money remained with which to continue the sinking of the shaft. But he persistently held onto his interest and his faith in the Enterprise Mine.

He continued to sink the shaft as fast as his finances would permit. He sold his saloon and put the proceeds into the mine, and he went heavily in debt besides. Yet no ore showed.

His wife, Laura, who ran a boarding house in Rico, was loyal and had boundless faith in him. On several occasions when he was greatly discouraged and ready to quit. she gave her encouragement in a practical form by putting the small earnings from her boarding house into the Enterprise. She even begrudged the dollar credit she gave a transient boarder on his bill in payment for a ticket in the Louisiana Lottery she bought from him. And still no ore showed in the Enterprise shaft!

Time slipped by and with it conditions became more difficult and more discouraging for Swickheimer. In addition to bad luck due to lack of experience in mining operations, and to floods of water, finances were almost exhausted. To add to his difficulties Larned and Hackett were rapidly drifting northwest on a vein on an adjoining claim which overlapped onto the Enterprise, and threatened to reach the boundary line separating the two properties; unless Barlow and Swickheimer succeeded in finding a mineral-bearing vein in place on their claim so as to permit a valid location, their right to the property could be successfully disputed by Larned and Hackett whenever the latter reached the line.

And then something happened: a check for $2500 came in the mail to Mrs. Swickheimer! Her ticket in the Louisiana Lottery had been the winning number! With this amount of capital, so providentially provided, Swickheimer was enabled to work on the Enterprise shaft.

And still no ore was found! All of the lottery money, except enough for one more shift, had been spent in the shaft apparently to no avail.

In utter despair and abject despondency, Swickheimer felt

43

forced to quit. And again Mrs. Swickheimer came to his rescue. She persuaded him to continue—at least for one more shift, even though the expense would take their last thin dime. Grudgingly Swickheimer agreed. The last shift went on. The miners drilled the holes, loaded them with dynamite and set off the final blast; and on October 6, 1887, at a depth of 262 feet, he broke into a flat body of rich gold and silver ore—the famous Enterprise blanket vein of which no previous knowledge had existed.

Good Luck! The Goddess of Good Luck had both her arms around Swickheimer and even in the dreariest hours of his discouragements she was guiding the immutable forces that brought him success!

Later developments showed that had the Enterprise shaft been located only a few feet farther east, it would have been beyond the outer edge of the blanket vein and would have missed that rich formation completely. The shaft would have been a blank dud. And if Mrs. Laura Swickheimer had not bought a lottery ticket, grudgingly though she did, the indispensable finances so vital to ultimate success would not have been available!

A short straw, a woman's faith and encouragement, and one man's persistent tenacity led to the discovery of an exceptional geological freak formation that yielded millions in treasure, made Rico famous, and made Swickheimer a millionaire.

(Parenthetically speaking: After several years of profitable production Swickheimer was paid the fantastic sum of $1,250,000 in cash for his interest in the Enterprise mine. This was in May, 1890. By following the blanket deposit struck in the Enterprise shaft in the fall of 1886, Swickheimer encountered the true fissure vein, from which the blanket had come, in July, 1888, and by reason of this discovery, the Enterprise then became a real mine. By 1895 its underground workings had extended eight miles in length, with comparable stopes, had employed a force of 500 men, and by this date had produced ore of the gross value of $3,500,000. One-fourth of the ore values was in gold and the balance was silver.)

Stolen Bullion of Indian Ridge

Safely cached away deep in the spruce forest adjacent to the Burnt Timber flats on Indian ridge, is a tidy little fortune of $40,000 in the richest gold ore ever mined in the La Plata mountains. I helped to put it there years ago, when I was a teenage boy, and there it still remains.

During the summer seasons of 1909, 1910, and 1911, I was the foreman, caporal, and packer on my father's sheep outfit on the Hermosa side of the Indian ridge a few miles east of the mining and railroad town of Rico, Colorado. The Indian ridge was the name given to the divide between the watersheds of the Hermosa and the Dolores rivers. It butted squarely up against the Cumberland basin at the head of the La Plata river and extended north about 40 miles to the Spanish peaks at the head of the Hermosa. This was a wild and untamed country then as now, uninhabited by anyone except an occasional stockman in the summer season, and by no one at all during the snowy wintertime.

Along the ridge ran an old Indian trail used by the Utes generations before the coming of the white men. It was one of my jobs to pack stock salt from the May Day switch, a spur on the Rio Grande Southern railroad, on the La Plata river up over this old abandoned trail to our sheep outfit. It took a lot of salt for 7000 ewes and their lambs, eating the fresh, green forage, so my trips after salt were very frequent.

The Rio Grande Southern, known in railroad circles as "The Little Giant," was a famous narrow-gauge line through the rugged mountain country of southwestern Colorado. It was the connecting link between Durango on the south and Ridgway on the north, but between these two points it made a wide circuitous swing west to the Dolores river and followed up that rugged mountain canyon to the famous mining camps of Rico, Ophir, Telluride, and others. The line of the railroad from May Day switch to Rico had about the same relation to the trail I followed as a bow would have to its string. The Indian trail was a cut-off between the two points.

The May Day switch was located on the Bar, a wide tableland on the west side of the La Plata river, opposite the famous mine of that name. A short distance up-river was the equally rich and famous Idaho mine. Both of these diggings were in plain view of the switch, and many were the miners that watched "the kid," as I was known, come and go with his pack string of burros. And on different occasions, the kid saw miners stealing furtively along in the twilight through the scattered clumps of scrub oak, with a small sack of highgrade over their shoulders, to conceal it somewhere. Sometimes, when I was rounding up my jacks to pack them, I would accidentally find one of these caches where the wind had blown the protecting cover of oak leaves off it, but since I wanted to live a long life and not be crippled in the beginning of it, I very carefully left them alone. To molest some other man's highgrade was serious business, and I knew it. I did not want any serious business.

"Highgrade" and "highgrading" are technical terms known to the mining industry wherever rich ore is mined. Highgrading is the practice engaged in by some of the workmen of sorting out and appropriating to their own use and profit many of the richest pieces of ore they can get away with. In short, it is stealing ore. The ore so taken is "highgrade," but is usually known to the trade in each district by some local term. In the La Plata quadrangle is was called "grommets," while over at Creede the local term was "rubies," and in Telluride it was "mocha" and "java."

Highgrading was a crime punishable by fine and imprisonment if a man got caught. But in those days the chances of getting caught were not very great after a man got his grommets out of the locality and marketed. To get them way from the immediate vicinity of the mine was the most difficult problem. And that is where I came in.

Early one September morning in 1910, I was loading my pack string with salt at the switch, preparatory to getting off on my long trek back into the mountains. A fellow came over to talk to me. He was a big man, over six feet tall and proportionately broad. He was all bone and muscle. To a kid like me he looked

46

like a giant. He said he was a miner from one of the nearby mines.

"You have a good string of pack jacks," he remarked.

"Yes. I do," I replied. "I have to, to get this stuff through to where I'm going."

"And where is that?" he asked.

When I told him it was on the Indian ridge almost up to the old Rico toll road, he got very interested. He asked me a lot of questions about the country. He inquired where the various trails turned off the Indian Ridge on the Dolores side toward the Rio Grande railroad, and then he asked me, "Kid, how would you like to make $50?"

"I'd like it fine," I replied. I had a hunch right then what the job was to be.

"Can you keep your mouth shut?" he asked.

"For $50 I can be absolutely deaf, dumb, and blind," I answered.

"Good enough," he responded. "This is what I want you to do. I have a load of stuff down here that I want you to pack over to Rico for me. I'll go along with you. There will be about 800 pounds in the lot, so bring along enough jacks to pack that amount without loading anyone of them very heavy. We may want to travel fast. Bring a saddle horse for me, and be here just about dark a week from tonight. I'll meet you somewhere along this road between here and the mouth of the canyon and show you where to go."

I came back with my pack string at the proper hour on the evening specified, and sure enough, my man, known as Long John, met me on the road some little distance above the switch. We turned off the road at this point and traveled about 200 yards westward through the oak brush. Here we found another man standing guard over a pile of sacks of grommets. Long John explained to me that this man was his partner and that the sacks of ore were the stuff they wanted me to move.

"There are 12 sacks altogether," he said, "and they weigh about 70 pounds apiece, so now you know how to figure your loads. But be damn sure and tie them on securely, 'cause we do not want to lose any of them; and let us get busy and get out of here, pronto."

Both men were nervous and on the alert. The partner did nothing but stand over near the edge of the little clearing, with his rifle across his arm, peering into the twilight and listening for the sound of approaching feet. Long John tried to help me load the burros, but he knew nothing about packing and was more of a hindrance than a help. But it did not take me long to do the loading. In about 20 minutes we were ready to go. As we pulled out in the deepening twilight and headed north into the darkness of the La Plata canyon, I heard his partner say to Long John: "I'll meet you at the other end of the line."

Long John and I traveled all night with that burro string. We got out of the La Plata canyon and over the highest and most rugged part of Indian ridge. Daylight found us back down to timberline at the head of South Roaring fork. We decided to camp there for the day to let our stock rest and to get some sleep ourselves. As we were unloading, Long John said to me, "Listen, kid. I ain't fooling you a bit, and I know it. You know that this stuff we are packing off here is highgrade ore, and you are right. It is the richest ore out of the richest mine in the La Platas. Me and my pardner have been a long time in getting it together, and now we don't want to lose it. I want to hide these sacks for the short while we are camped here. Each one of them is worth better than $2000 and I ain't a-kiddn' you." (And that was at the old price of gold. Add 75% for the current value.)

"That is easy," I replied. "Just throw each jack's saddle and blankets over his load as we unsaddle them and when we get through there will be nothing in sight but the empty saddles."

I did not doubt Long John's estimation of value in the slightest degree. In fact, I thought it rather modest, because I knew that ore had been taken out of both the May Day and the Idaho worth $50 a pound. I deeply regretted that I did not have a major interest in that $40,000 batch of highgrade. I was sorry that I was not a highgrader.

Two mornings later we broke timber on the edge of Burnt Timber flats, where the trail from Monteloros switch on the Rio Grande Southern came out on top of the ridge and joined ours. There was Long John's partner waiting for us. He had come around on the train to that siding and had walked up the hill to intercept us. Long John was greatly surprised to see him. I had a hunch that all was not going as planned.

The two men held a rather earnest conference at a point too far away for me to hear what was said, but when it was over they approached me and Long John said:

"We won't take this stuff any farther now, kid. 'Taint safe. We want to hide it back here in the timber somewhere and wait until the excitement dies down. You stay here while me and my pardner take the jacks back a little way and unload them."

How far back into that dense forest those two men went I do not know. They were gone about three hours. They cached the ore, however, because the burros were unloaded when they came back. Long John gave me a specimen of the ore for a keepsake along with the $50 he paid me for packing the ore that far. I have that specimen yet. It was about the size of half a walnut and contained far more gold than it did quartz. An assayer told me later that the specimen itself was worth almost as much as the money Long John paid me.

Long John and his partner went their way down the hill to take the train back to their jobs. Before we parted they assured me that they would return at no distant date to move their treasure on to market, and made me promise to help them again at that time with my pack stock. I went on about my own business and was extremely occupied during the balance of the autumn. An early snow during the equinoctial storm in the high country made it necessary to move the sheep out of the mountains early that year.

I did not take the time to return to Burnt Timber flat immediately and try to locate the place of the cache, and I was not inclined to do so. I would not have known how to dispose of the ore if I had possessed it, and I certainly would have received no cooperation from my father or from my older brother. I would have gotten a good "jacking up" instead. So I did nothing about it.

I could have found the very spot where the ore was buried had I turned my attention to the search immediately, before the tracks of the burros and the men became obliterated by the storm. I could have tracked the pack jacks to the point where the men unloaded them, and I could have tracked the men to the place where they buried the ore. It might have been a painstaking task for a few hours, but I could have done it successfully. In the light of subsequent events I have deeply regretted that I did not do it.

I did not return to the mountains with the sheep the following summer. I heard indirectly that some big, broad-shouldered man had made inquiries for me at some of the camps, but that was all. I knew it was Long John, and I wondered how he finally succeeded in getting his ore packed out, and how much money he realized out of it. That he would not be able to find his cache never entered my mind.

It had all seemed so logical, so reasonable, and so natural to me that I did not think of any difficulty in connection with the ore except the rather minor one of transportation. The caching of highgrade ore, until a favorable time to carry it away, was a common practice, and I had never before known of a miner being unable to find his treasure. Imagine my surprise, and my regrets, when a few years later I found Long John in a Boulder, Colorado, sanitarium. He was in the last stages of miner's consumption. The following is his story:

"When my pardner came to us on the flats that morning, he said we were under suspicion and that it was not safe to go on with our ore just then. We did not want to take the chances on going to the pen and of having our highgrade confiscated at the same time, so we determined to hide it out and lie low until the next summer.

"When we took those burros and went back into the forest, we did not follow the trail you and I came out by. We just headed back into the timber, winding our way through the fallen logs and around the boggy places.

"I would guess we traveled between a quarter and a half of a mile before we found a place to our liking for our cache. The soil was soft and easy to work at this point, so we dug a long trench, about two feet deep, and put our sacks of grommets in the bottom of it and covered them up. We did a good job, too. We tramped all the dirt back into that trench on top of those sacks. Then we smoothed the place over and scattered some old leaf mold over it in such a way that it could not be distinguished from any of the rest of the surrounding ground.

50

"We did not want to leave any artificial marks around there so we did not cut any blazes on the tree near the cache, but we marked the place by natural objects in such a way we were sure we could go back to it. From it we could see the bluff on a hillside across the Dolores river. South of the cache about 50 yards was a tall dead tree with a peculiarly twisted branch at the top. To the westward was a little spring. A few feet southwest of the trench my pardner stuck a small dead limb, branches pointing down, in the ground. He set it at an angle so it would look like it had fallen there naturally, but we were sure we would recognize it when we saw it again. About the same distance on the opposite side, I laid a piece of dead sapling, about seven feet long and five or six inches through, across the upturned roots of a dead log. I put it there in such a way that one end of the stick jutted out beyond the roots quite a bit more than the other. We would recognize that when we saw it again, too.

"Maybe we would have found the place, if my pardner had been along with me, but he got killed in a mining accident in Arizona the winter before. I went up there alone the next summer, but I could never find the place, nor the markings we had left. I got so confused I could hardly find my way back out of the timber. I tried to find you, but you were gone and the Mexican sheepherders could not tell me where you were. I finally had to give up the search and come away, and I have never been back since.

"Kid," continued the old man, "that fortune is still there. Right where me and my pardner buried it. We never told another soul about it, and it is worth going after, and it is yours if you can find it. My pardner is already gone and I soon will be, so it won't ever do us any good. It might pay you big to hunt for it, and I wish you the best of luck."

And with those few remarks, Long John started me on a fascinating lost treasure hunt that has extended intermittently through the years. I have not found the treasure yet, but always there is the furtive hope that on the next trip the powerful forces of nature may be kind enough to settle the covering soil over that trench enough to show a marked depression, or to wash one little corner of it away, leaving exposed the frayed and rotted fragment of a telltale canvas ore bag.

In all my searching I have had the satisfaction of knowing that I was hunting for a cache whose existence was not clouded in doubt, veiled in mystery, or complicated with legend. The story of it has never before been told, so as yet there has not sprung up about it the usual crop of legends. What happened to those markers is not difficult for a man familiar with mountain winters to understand. Violent winter storms are of frequent occurrence in this district, and snow accumulated to a depth of five to seven feet. The sapling that Long John laid across the old log became overbalanced with snow and fell off from the perch on which he had put it, and possibly in the violence of the winter tempests that occur in that country, it had been thrown several feet from the log on which he put it; while the small branch which his partner had so carefully planted on an angle like it had fallen naturally, became overbalanced with a burden of snow and had fallen flat on the ground to undergo some disintegration during the winter season and thus to be so altered in appearance by natural forces as to be unrecognizable in the spring. The tree with the peculiar top could undergo similar changes from the heavy snowfall or violent winds by having a limb broken off, or a peculiar knot removed by nature which would be sufficient to change its appearance. To any man familiar with the forces of nature in the mountain country, and cognizant of the fickle character of natural marking of this sort, such changes are not surprising or unusual. In fact they are to be expected, but Long John and his partner, being unfamiliar with the out-of-door conditions, were like many other neophytes and accepted as permanent their puny efforts in making futile markings that were so susceptible to alteration by the common forces of snow and wind. They wrote their marking upon the sands of circumstances and the elements erased their writings. The irresistible forces of nature so altered their artificial "open sesame" to their golden treasure, that Long John could not discern the combination to the natural safe deposit box in which they deposited their rich treasure, nor have I, as yet, been able to interpret the changes that nature wrought; but I have not yet given up hope.

The unalterable existence of Burnt Timber flats, the cache of ore nearby, and the bluff on the mountain side across the Dolores river have successfully withstood the ravages of time and silently guard a fortune in gold in the stately forest on the famous Ridge.

The Lost Estes Mine

Tom Estes was a miner and prospector in the San Juan mountains of southwestern Colorado, in the early nineties. He knew his rocks and rills. Several men since then have wished they knew the "rocks" as well as Estes did.

Estes arrived at the cow camp of his friend Doff Lusk on the Cascade creek one autumn evening about the year 1893. He had come from the West Needle Mountains, and had brought along, on one of his pack horses, two sacks of very rich sylvanite ore.

"I sure hit it this time, Doff," he told his friend after the usual formal greetings had been made.

"I am glad to hear that," replied Doff, "and I hope you've struck it big."

"I've got it, both big and rich," Estes said. "I'll show you some of my ore just as soon as I can get it unpacked. It'll make your eyes stick out. A lot of it is half gold."

At this juncture in the proceedings Lusk's two nephews came up to where the men were talking. They were staying with their uncle and helping him with the cattle. Kid-like they became very interested in what was going on.

When the horses were unpacked and hobbled out for the night, Estes opened his sacks of ore for his friend's inspection. Neither Lusk nor his nephews were mining men, but it did not require much knowledge of ore to convince anyone that this was indeed rich. Gold was not so scarce in those days; everyone knew the metal when he saw it. There was plenty of it to be seen in Tom's ore.

Lusk and his two kid nephews gawked in amazement when they beheld the ore.

"You sure got a fortune there, Tom, if you have very much of that," exclaimed Lusk.

"Well, I got it," replied Estes, "got an eight inch streak of that ore in place."

"How much will you get for these two sacks?" asked the two boys almost in unison.

"I'll get a thousand dollars if I get a nickel," replied Estes.

"What!" exclaimed Lusk, almost incredulously, "why those sacks won't weigh 50 pounds apiece."

"I know they won't. But it don't take much gold to be worth a lot of money."

During the remainder of the evening, Estes' mine and his ore were a topic of frequent conversation. It was a very exciting affair, especially so to the two boys, Harry and Dell McWilliams. Estes talked freely and frankly about his mine: how he had discovered it, what work he had done on it, and how he had concealed it; but he gave no information as to its location, other than to say it was somewhere on the southernly slopes of the West Needles.

"You could blame near see it from here," he said, "if you knew just where to look."

Lusk and Estes had been friends for years. The cow camp was located at the end of the wagon road into the mountains in those days. For several summers past it had been Tom's custom to bring his wagon as far as the camp, and leave it with his extra supplies, while he went on into the higher mountains with pack animals. He knew very well that whatever he told these fellows about his mine would not be repeated. The early cattleman knew how to keep a secret. Even their children were taught the value of silence. To them the keeping of a secret was a matter of sacred honor.

The following morning Estes loaded up his wagon and went on his way. As he went out of sight around a bend in the road, Lusk remarked rather wistfully to his nephews:

"I had a chance to be in on that mine."

"How was that, Uncle?" they asked.

"The old man wanted me to grubstake him, when he first came up here prospecting three years ago, but I would not do it. Now I wish I had done so."

"Gee! We would be rich now, if you had've done so, wouldn't we?"

"Yes, we would."

"We could follow him when he goes back next year and find out where it is," remarked the boys.

"No. I would not do that," said Lusk. "I passed up my chance. So I will let the matter go."

Nothing further was seen or heard of Estes, until the following June, when he again showed up at the cow camp on his way back to his mine. In answer to the query of how much he had received for his two sacks of ore, he replied:

"I got $1070 for 'em."

"I suppose," remarked Lusk, "you are going to dig out all the ore you can this summer, so you can cash in for a big wad this fall."

"No, I am not," replied Estes. "I am going to take out enough to make me a nice little stake, and that is all. I'll leave the rest of it in the hill, and go back and get it as I want it. It's safer there."

That he had something permanent to work on was shown by the fact that he brought along a goodly supply of tools, including an anvil, bellows, and some blacksmith's coal. All of these, together with his powder and several weeks supply of food, he loaded on his pack horses and set out for his mine.

After dusk that evening, the boys, Harry and Dell, saw a campfire high up near timberline, on the rough and rocky slopes of the West Needles.

"Some day," said Harry, "I am going to follow that old boy, and find out where that mine is."

"I'll be right with you," returned Dell.

Estes did not remain in the mountains as late as usual that summer. He returned to the cow camp, on his way out, about the middle of August. He brought with him seven sacks of rich ore. In conversation with Lusk that evening he gave the following information:

It had taken only two days of mining to take out those seven sacks of ore. The balance of the time he had spent in timbering the tunnel, in covering over a shaft he had sunk nearby during previous years, and in building a forge among some adjacent, big rocks. He had not built a blacksmith shop, nor had he built a cabin. Such things would attract attention. He had fixed up a permanent camping place, however, and had begun the construction of a foot path from this point to his tunnel.

After he had gone the next day, the two boys decided to back track him to the mine. Due to the topography of the country, there is only one way in which it is possible to get into the southern slopes of the West Needles; and that way is to take the regular trail down into Purgatory Canyon, leaving the trail at some point down there, and picking a way up the forbidding mountainside on the north.

The boys had no difficulty in following Estes' tracks until they got into the very rocky strip some little distance up the hill on the north side of Purgatory Canyon. From this point on their progress was so slow that they finally had to give it up for that day and return to camp. They had followed him far enough, however, to be absolutely certain he had come from the West Needles. By no means had they permanently abandoned their search, but they had no further opportunity to finish it that year. They planned to follow Estes in, when he came back in the spring.

It was almost mid-summer, however, before he returned the next year. Lusk and Dell, the younger boy, were away when Estes came to the cow camp, but Harry was there. When Estes left for his mine the next morning, Harry followed him. The tracks being fresh, he had very little trouble in trailing the old man through the rough country across Purgatory Canyon. He paused in the edge of the timber high up on the north side to look over the open and broken area ahead of him. He was sure Estes had preceded him through that rocky waste land. His thoughts were broken into by someone speaking to him from behind:

"What the Hell are you doing here?"

Guiltily Harry turned in his saddle to face the old man, who had been hidden behind a clump of brush. He was very angry and held his Winchester in a very menacing manner. He did not wait for a reply but continued:

"I told you never to follow me. When I get over here, all friendship ceases. I'll shoot any man I see break out of this timber, and I'll do the same with you, if you don't go back. Now get going."

And Harry "got going" on the back trail without arguing the matter.

Estes did not stay in the mountains very long this time. He came back to the cow camp within two weeks, but contrary to his usual custom, he did not stay all night there. He seemed to be in a hurry. He brought five sacks of ore and his camp outfit. In changing his packs from the horses to his wagon, he remarked he had forgotten his Dutch oven and had left it "over the hill."

At the cow camp Estes picked up an acquaintance of his by the name of Sim Hendrixon. This man was a local cow puncher, prospector, and miner. He was quite well known in the country. During the summer months he would prospect and mine, but he would get a job punching cows on some outfit during the winter.

On their way to town he asked Estes for a small loan. Estes promised to make the loan just as soon as he sold his ore, and he invited Hendrixon to accompany him when he went to make the sale. Hendrixon did, and he is authority for the following:

"Estes got $2800 for those five sacks of ore. I saw him get it, and he loaned me $100 of it before he ever put it in his pocket."

That was the last ore Estes ever took out. He died of pneumonia the following winter without leaving any intelligible maps or directions by which his mine could be found. When he realized he was going to die, he tried hard to tell where his mine was, and how to discover it, but the people to whom he was talking knew nothing about the mountains and got things so confused that what information they had was useless. On the basis of that information, men have hunted for those lost diggings on Lime Creek, around Engineer mountain, and as far away as South Mineral Creek.

It was several years before the news of Estes' death, and the fact that he had left a rich mine, got spread around. The Mc-Williams boys did not return to the Cascade with the cattle the following years, so they did not miss the old man. When they did hear of his death, they had grown to manhood, and immediately determined to look for the mine. Other men had already been doing the same thing.

In their searching the boys found Estes' Dutch oven, a permanent camping place, and a shallow shaft that had once been covered over. Hendrixon found an old forge built in amongst some big rocks, but no one has found any tools or tunnel as yet.

What happened? Did the old man leave his tools in the tunnel and conceal the portal so skillfully that no one can detect its location? He brought ore out of that country and he certainly did not pack it in there from somewhere else before bringing it out. His source of supply was in there some place, and there it still remains just as he left it. How much there is of it, no one actually knows, but there are many of us in this country who would certainly like to be the lucky ones in getting the first-hand information.

The Lost Carson Mine

The history of the great Southwest is replete with yarns and legends of lost mines and hidden treasures. Most of these tales have their origins in the remote past and are associated with the exploits of the early Spaniards in America. Many of the stories are obscure in origin and location and have been embellished through the decades with fanciful details supplied by the fertile imagination of the narrators. This is not the case, however, with the fabulously rich bonanza discovered by Levi Carson in the early 90's in the rough, mountainous country near the rip-roaring, tumultuous, mining town of Silverton, Colorado.

Carson was only one of many prospectors in this rich district where several big mines had already been discovered and were making their owners rich with their amazing production of gold and silver ores. He did not attract any extraordinary attention from the populace, nor did he receive any treatment not accorded to all other prospectors in the area. No one took any special interest in his activities. He was only one of the crowd until—

He came into Silverton in September, 1895, bringing two of his burros loaded with extremely rich gold ore, to the value of $2800 worth in four ordinary ore-bags! This event made him a marked man and an outstanding character. Everyone took notice of him after that and began to elicit an intense interest in his welfare and his activities—especially his activities. This undue solicitude irked the old man. He highly resented it. He wanted to be left alone and to be treated in the same way he had been before he "struck it rich." He had always been a taciturn figure, not very communicative, solitary, and highly individualistic. Very little was known about his past life. He attended to his own affairs and left other people to attend to theirs. He had his own outfit of tools, burros, and camp equipment, and he always prospected alone. Partners were not a part of his program; nor did he go into the sections where many prospectors were to be found. He often remarked: "Other fellers in a locality makes things too public. It leads to arguments, causes quarrels, and develops friction. When a man is out by hisself he hain't got no body around telling him where gold is and where it ain't. He can foller his own judgment without havin' to fuss with anybody else about it."

When Carson started out to prospect, he would load his provisions and equipment on his own burros and pull out into the rougher and more remote parts of the mountains. Here in secrecy and solitude he would carry on his search. Many times he would be gone for a month or more without anyone seeing him or knowing anything about his whereabouts—or caring anything about him. He would be seen occasionally coming into town, or going out, but further than that no one knew where he went or what direction he took.

And no one knew from what direction he had come on that September afternoon when he arrived at a Silverton smelter with his cargoes of amazingly rich ore. He had so timed his arrival at the plant that he would find it open for business. He stopped at the refinery on his way into town and unloaded his four sacks of ore. He took a receipt for them and said he would return later, after the samples were run, to make settlement.

Carson's ore was so exceptional and was so extremely rich in native gold that it amazed the veteran assayer who sampled it at the smelter. It was so rich that the assayer could not believe the results of his first assay. He felt sure he had made an error somewhere in his work, so he ran a second sample to check on the results of the first one. He was astounded when the results of the second confirmed the first, yet could not believe that the ore was so rich. He ran a third sample to check on the other two. Not until the outcome of this assay confirmed the results of the other two was he convinced that he had made no mistake in his work and that the ore was actually so astonishingly rich. The assayer brought the extraordinary incident to the attention of the officials of the smelting company.

These men were waiting for Carson when he came back to get his money late that afternoon. They wanted information about the property, about the location of the district in which Carson had got the ore, with a view of promoting further prospecting in the area. They offered to purchase the property from Carson. He refused. Then they offered to "grubstake" him for an interest in the mine. Again he refused. He emphatically refused to reveal the location of his mine or of the district in which he had made his discovery. To all their propositions he firmly replied: "I don't need any grubstake, and I don't need anybody's money, and I ain't goin' to take any. I got all I want and more, too, where this came from. I can go and get all I need whenever I want it, and as I want it. And cain't no body argue with me about it. I am satisfied with things as they are and I aim to keep 'em that way."

The company paid him for his ore. It is said he received over $2800 for the four sacks which weighed about 200 pounds. Later in the evening he displayed one roll of bills containing $700 which he said was a part of the money he had been paid for his ore. Whether this amount was the total proceeds or the pay for one sack is less important than the fact that four sacks of rich ore had been brought into town from "somewhere" and had actually been sold. This concrete fact made tangible proof of the existence of a vein somewhere thereabouts, and definitely eliminated the nebulous cloud of legend and fancy that obscured other reported "discoveries."

Carson's ore was different from any other that had been discovered in the Silverton district up to that date, which fact led mining men and other prospectors to conclude it had come from some locality where little or no prospecting had been done. It was an oxide ore in a brownish, sugar quartz, and thoroughly impregnated with coarse, free gold. Many of the particles were as large as grains of wheat. No magnifying glass was necessary to see the yellow metal in that quartz.

Nothing spreads faster than news of a rich gold strike in a mining district. It travels even faster than a choice bit of scandalous gossip in a small community. Within an hour or two after Carson had received his pay for the ore, his fabulous discovery was the talk of the town. Specimens of his ore saved out at the smelter were quite freely shown and were carefully studied and compared by all prospectors and miners who saw them. Carson himself proudly showed several specimens that he had kept for that purpose.

Where he had made his strike was the question uppermost in everyone's mind. The old prospector was besieged with inquiries about the location of the district in which he made his discovery; but he very discreetly refused to divulge any useful information in reply to these questions. He was profusely "wined" and dined, especially wined, in the hopes that when he got a bit drunk he would lose his discretion and would let slip some tell-tale remark. Carson liked to drink, and it is said he got pretty well "lit up" on this occasion, but he always had one stock reply to all these questions about "where," and that was, "You go find out for yourself. That is what I done."

Carson was in no hurry to return to his mine, wherever it was located. He had plenty of money to meet all his needs, so why rush back to get more ore? He spent several days in Silverton "celebrating." Saloons and gambling halls were numerous in that booming mining town at that time, and Carson patronized them all—especially the saloons. It was said of him on this occasion that "he never got drunk, but he did get comfortably full," which was defined as being a sort of gentleman's degree of intoxication.

He was prudent, however, because when his "celebration" ended he had plenty of money left and had provided himself generously with food and clothing for the winter. He had also bought a generous sized jug of whiskey to take with him when he should leave town. His preparation for departure was very carefully watched by several different men. Since he had consistently refused to divulge any information about the location of his rich bonanza, some fellows determined to follow him and find the location in that way. This, they figured, would be easy and would be the most certain way in which to get the job done.

If Carson had any suspicions that anyone intended to follow him, he showed no signs of it. Just at the edge of dusk one evening he hired an express wagon and had its driver haul his supplies down to the grassy meadow near the ball park south of town where he had his burros hobbled out on pasture. He rounded up his jacks and remained there for the night, but before daylight next morning he had his stuff loaded on his burros and pulled out over the old toll road around the rugged slopes of Mt. Snowden toward Big Molas lake.

At the upper end of this long grade on the heavily timbered flat near the old John Herr cabin, Carson did a very strange thing. He left the wagon road and turned off into the dense spruce timber on the east side of it. This was a long wide bench of comparatively level country as such places go in the mountains. It extended for over three miles south from this place to a point beyond Big Molas lake. A long, narrow meadow lay along the western side of this bench for two thirds of its length, and terminated on its southern end around the lake. The eastern three quarters of this mesa, the area between the meadow on one side and the edge of the deep Animas canyon on the other, was covered with a magnificent stand of spruce timber. This was one small section that had escaped being burned in the great forest fire, known as the big Lime Creek Burn, in 1878-79.

Carson spent the day traveling through this short strip. He circled around in the area, doubled back on his tracks frequently, crisscrossed the bench several times, and generally acted in a mighty puzzling manner. But if he saw anyone following him, he did not betray the fact. He camped about sundown that evening in a secluded nook on a grassy bench on the slope south of Molas lake toward Snowflake creek, not more than six miles from town. His camp was so well concealed on this spot that a man would be almost right at it before he realized the fact. If Carson saw a couple of surprised human figures suddenly duck back out of sight when they saw his camp, he did not let on. He calmly continued to prepare his supper and make ready to spend the night.

For a man trying to conceal his course of travel, Carson's actions the following morning were even more mysterious than the day before. When he broke camp that morning he pulled directly out into the long, open valley of Snowflake creek and headed directly across that grassy meadow for the high divide between it and East Lime creek. True this valley was not immediately adjacent to places of public travel, but certainly it afforded no concealment. Anyone interested in his movements

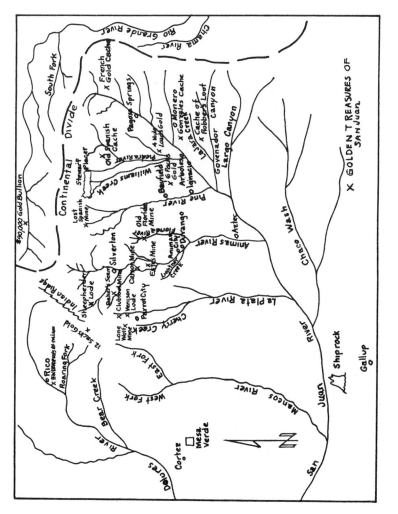

Sketch Map of Treasure Caches in San Juan

65

View up La Plata Canyon and high range close to Parrott Peak.

Parrott Peak on the La Plata River. Location Lone Wolf, Lost Clubfoot, and Milt Hollingsworth's Venison Lode.

View of La Plata City in 1894 near the headwaters of La Plata River.

Big Blaze to mark vicinity of Club Foot mine.

Clubfoot Mine area. Somewhere in the timber. Cornelius in the foreground.

Root Gulch. Clubfoot territory.

La Plata Canyon where Milt Hollingsworth found Venison Lode.

Rico, Colorado, in 1880.

Enterprise million dollar blanket. First dump top center is Newman Hill. Enterprise Shaft was on flat area. Town is Rico, Colorado, in 1920's. *Walker Studios, Montrose.*

71

Lost Estes Mine (Silverton), West Needles.

Lost Carson Mine. View of West Needles looking down Lime Creek from Million Dollar highway.

could easily and safely have observed his progress across this area from any one of a number of higher points and ridges surrounding the beautiful mountain basin.

Carson's efforts to hide his flight and to confuse his pursuers, if he had any, must have seemed very absurd and ineffectual to them. Already he had spent one full day in aimlessly wandering around in a short strip of forest, but had really done nothing effective to throw anyone off his trail; and here he was on the second morning making his trek across open country. This conduct would seem like the merest child-play to anyone experienced in mountain travel. If this was the best he could do, following him to his rich mine would be easy. All it would require would be patience and persistence. It wouldn't even require skill in tracking or in concealment.

If any such thoughts occurred to Carson, they did not bother him. He methodically went his way, nor did he have any great amount of difficulty in threading his way with his burros through the mass of fallen logs and dead timber that covered a wide strip of the divide over which he had to travel to get to East Lime creek. This ridge had been heavily timbered at the time of the big burn in '78. The forest fire of that year had burned over this area along with the rest of the Lime creek regions. Now the divide was covered with a tangled mass of fallen logs that made travel through there with packstock almost impossible. There were no trails cleared through the area. Carson, however, got through with a minimum of difficulty. He seemed to be familiar with the locality.

Once across this difficult area, Carson had smooth traveling down the long, narrow valley or vega along the banks of East Lime creek. This strip was a natural mountain meadow not covered with timber at the time of the big fire; so it was free of down timber and was smooth and afforded easy traveling. The toll road, which he had left the previous day, ran along the bench north of this meadow at an acute angle. Gradually the two approached each other until they came together about four miles down stream near the canyon of Big Lime creek. When Carson got to this point, he turned his burros onto the wagon road and followed that thoroughfare down the long grade to the banks of

Lime creek proper. To say the least, open travel on a public road is a poor way to achieve concealment!

But at the foot of this grade, Carson did another peculiar thing. At this point the wagon road made a sharp turn and ran down the Lime Creek valley parallel to the stream bed. Opposite this bend and between it and the creek itself were some large rocks and a long narrow bench, covered with high willows, on the river bank. This bench extended upstream for two hundred yards. There were open patches between the clumps of willows, but these were not visible from the road nor from the main trail that left the road at the switchback to go up into the high mountains at the head of Lime creek, to a number of mines that were operating in those mountains at that time.

Carson turned his burros off of the road at the switchback and headed them down onto this willowed bench. He led them through the brush to the upper end of it and tied them securely with their halter ropes. He and his outfit were so completely hidden here from outside observation that they might just as well have fallen in a well. They just simply and effectively dropped out of sight, and in the silence of that beautiful autumn day, out of hearing. Carson was very careful and deliberate in his actions. He tied his burros well apart so they could not get tangled up with each other and start a commotion. He gave each of them an affectionate pat before he left them, and then stealthily slipped back to conceal himself in a clump of willows behind a big rock not ten feet from the turn in the road.

Presently he heard the thud of human feet coming down the road, and a few minutes later he heard a man, not twenty feet away, speak to his companion. "He ain't in sight nowhere," remarked the first voice. "Which way you reckon he went?"

"I dunno', mebbe up Lime creek," replied the second man.

"Let's see if his tracks head up the trail that way."

And the two men approached the main trail not over five feet from where Carson was hidden.

"What tracks you lookin' for?" demanded Carson as he stepped out directly in front of the two!

The two men were so surprised and so startled by this sudden and unexpected appearance of their quarry from out of "nowhere," that they could not answer him immediately.

Carson recognized both fellows. They were acquaintances he had made in Silverton the past few days, erstwhile prospectors, and had been most persistent in trying to learn from him the location of his rich strike.

"We thought you'd gone up Lime creek," one of them blurted out before he had time to collect his wits.

"Fooled you, didn't I?" remarked Carson, and his keen blue eyes appraised the other men with a cold and cutting expression. "I travel on my own thinkin' not anybody else's, and that goes for the future, too. You thought you would foller me and find out somethin', didn't you? Well, you have. You've found out I stopped here. Now get to hell outta here while you are still able, and don't try to foller me again. There is the back trail. Git! and git fast." If Carson was armed he did not display any gun to prove the fact. He didn't need to, because his two pursuers, chagrined, embarrassed, and scared, "got" back up the road the way they had come. Carson sat on the big rock and watched them go until they disappeared around a turn in the road.

Then he went back and got his burros and continued on his way down to the lower country, somewhere around Mancos, to spend the winter. He had not been on his way to his mine in the first place. He had plenty of money to winter on without going back to take out any more ore that season; so he was then leaving the mountains for the winter.

Carson did not show up in Silverton early the following spring much to the disappointment of a number of people who were watching for him. It was only natural, they reasoned, for a man who had a rich mine to be eager to get to work on it at the earliest possible date that weather conditions would permit. But when Carson tarried, people became mystified, and some were downright dubious about the whole thing.

Interest in his strike was suddenly and dramatically revived, however, late in the summer when he again appeared in Silverton just as dramatically and as mysteriously as he had done the year before. No one had seen him anywhere in the vicinity or had even suspected that he was anywhere about when he unexpectedly showed up with another cargo of his rich ore!

It was all very mystifying. How could he do it? How could a man so well known, and so eagerly watched for, get into the district, mine two burro loads of ore, and then transport that ore on his own pack string all the way into town, and yet not be seen by anyone while he was doing all this? He could not just materialize out of nowhere as a spirit being would, because Carson was no spirit. He was very tangible, very human, and very much a part of this world. So were his burros and the ore he brought along was very real. It was no myth or figment of the imagination. It was "the pure quill." It was just as rich as the ore he had sold the year before, and it was the same character of quartz. It had come from the same vein as the other had, but where was that vein?

"That is a million dollar secret," remarked one grizzly old prospector when asked his opinion about it, and in that one short sentence he expressed the collective opinion of the community.

Carson's second entry into Silverton was almost as electrifying as his first one was. Again he was the center of attention, especially among the less desirable element of the population. Rough miners in town for a holiday from work at active mines, unsuccessful prospectors, and plain ne'er-do-wells who were always seeking an opportunity to get something for nothing, were particularly attentive to the old man. Again he was beseiged with questions about the location of his bonanza, some of them were very adroit and cunning, but Carson was shrewd enough to evade them all. Again he was extensively "wined and dined," with him doing most of the paying and consuming copious quantities of the "wine." But he could "hold" his liquor. No matter how drunk he got he continued to be provokingly discreet about the location of his mine.

"He told nobody, nuthin'," was the laconic comment of one of his companions on the big spree.

He made no secret, however, of the fact that he had mined the ore on a property of his own somewhere in the environs of Silverton. He took delight in telling of the richness of the vein, and the fact that there was far more ore left than he had taken out.

"I gotta bank account there whenever I want to draw on it," he stated, "and more 'en I'll ever spend, an' so long as I keep its location a secret, ain't nobody going to take it away from me."

Several different men did their best to persuade Carson to let them accompany him on his return trip, pointing out to him that some accident might befall him while he was out in the mountains by himself; or that he might die suddenly and then the location of his mine would be lost to everyone.

Carson refused all these offers. He didn't need company, he said, he did not want company, and what was more he was not going to have company. He had been in the hills a whole lot by himself before and nothing had ever happened to him yet. He was still able to take care of himself without aid or assistance from anyone else, and "besides I ain't ready to die yet."

He summed up his statements by saying: "You fellers and me are friends here in town, but when I leave here all friendship ends. Don't try to go with me or to foller me, because if you do, you may not git back." And his listeners were convinced that he meant what he said.

In spite of his warning, however, one man did follow him. He found it a very difficult task, but by persistent effort he succeeded in ascertaining what direction Carson traveled when he left town. He discreetly shadowed the old prospector to a point several miles out on the Big Lime creek watershed. This had been a heavily timbered area before the big forest fire, but now, almost 20 years afterwards, it was denuded of live trees and was covered instead with a tangled mass of fallen logs and standing dead trees that might topple over any time. There were no trails in the area at that time, no cleared travelway to facilitate travel through the district. True, the old toll road between Silverton and Durango traversed this area, but Carson had not followed it on this occasion. He was threading his way with his burros through the loggy and rugged terrain on the long slope east of the road. No man would get out into such an uninviting bit of country as that unless he had a very impelling reason. Carson seemed to be familiar with the area. He was getting through it with a minimum of difficulty and apparently knew exactly how and where to guide his burros to get through. He was working his way up this slope toward a strip of live timber that had escaped the big fire, and which lay along the top of the divide between Lime creek and the Animas canyon.

This divide was a northern extension of the rugged West Needle mountains which lay a few miles away in the direction that Carson was traveling. Apparently that group of mountains was his goal. And no prospecting had ever been done in that area before!

Carson's pursuer decided against the risk of detection by openly following so closely behind the old man across this area. He determined, instead, to let the old prospector go on his way without immediate pursuit. He reasoned that with one day's traveling intervening, he would be much safer from detection but could still easily follow the tracks of the burros. He figured he just the same as had the cat in the bag. Carson, he concluded, having traveled this far into that remote region, without discovering that he was followed, would be less cautious and would go directly to his mine.

He had some difficulty the following day in tracking the burros over that rough and rocky terrain. It required pretty close attention to business to do it, but he succeeded, however, in following them a few miles into the back country along the divide. He was delighted with his success and inwardly elated that he had outwitted the old man. The rest of his task, he concluded, would be easy. With Carson several miles ahead, and with a covering of standing timber as a curtain to conceal him, all he had to do now, he thought, was to follow the trail that the old man had left. No need for undue caution. Such were the pursuer's musings as he topped a low ridge not more than half a mile after he had entered the live forest into which Carson had disappeared two evenings before. He was astounded and astonished at the sight before him! There were Carson's burros fully packed! They were quietly grazing in a secluded little park in the timber not more than a hundred feet from where he stood! Carson, however, was nowhere in sight. Before the man could recover from his astonishment at this unexpected situation and gather his wits together, he had a greater and more serious surprise. From a point about twenty-five feet behind him Carson, in a cold, sharp tone of voice, demanded: "What in hell you doin' here?"

Instantly the man realized he was trapped! He became panicky. He turned to face Carson, who had stepped out from concealment holding his Winchester menacingly in hand and ready for instant use.

"I didn't expect to find you here," he stammered too excited to think of any other excuse except the truth.

"I know you didn't. But I was expectin' you, I been waitin' for more'n an hour for you to git here."

Carson recognized the man as one he had seen in Silverton several times, but with whom he had not been familiar. He had never joined in Carson's drinking bouts but had been in conference with several of the other men who had. He was not of the two who had followed Carson the fall before.

"What are you following me for?" demanded Carson again.

"I didn't mean no harm, honest I didn't. A bunch of fellers in town hired me to trail you to see where you was agoin'."

"Where I'm agoin' ain't none o' nobody's business," blurted Carson. "But you come purty near going to hell just now, and it ain't too late for me to send you there yet. You mess with me any and I'll fill your worthless hide with lead."

"I ain't agoin' to mess with you," the fellow hastened to assure him. "If yu'll point that gun some other way and let me go, I swear I'll git outta here and stay out."

"And how about keepin' your mouth shut?" inquired Carson.

"I'll do that, too. I won't tell a soul nuthin, if yu'll let me go," promised the other fellow. In this tight spot the man had become an animated promissory note.

Carson, however, was not too easily satisfied and was in no mood to dismiss the situation lightly. The expression in his cold, blue eyes gave a lot of forceful meaning to his words as he said: "You better remember your promises, feller, and now get to hell outta here afore I start shooting. I'll give ye three minits to git outta sight."

The man started back-tracking pretty fast but not fast enough to suit Carson who began to pepper bullets at him. At any rate that is the story the man told many months later. He got back to

Silverton the following afternoon. His clothes were badly torn, and he was bruised and scratched up as the result of his precipitous flight through the logs and timber in getting away from Carson. He pointed to a round hole in his hat and another in his pantleg which he said were where a couple of Carson's bullets had passed. Other than that scant bit of information, he refused to comment. He was afraid to. He knew that if he did tell anything, Carson would be sure to find it out and do a better job of marksmanship next time. Not until long after Carson's death did the man tell what actually had happened. The information was of little value to anyone then.

Nothing was seen or heard of Carson for the following six weeks. Interest in him and his rich strike had begun to subside a little, when he made another of his dramatic appearances in Silverton with more ore to sell. He did not bring such a heavy cargo on this occasion. He had it in four sacks but the bags were only partly filled. "Just enough for a comfortable winter grubstake," he remarked. "I don't need no more'n that now." It was said that he received a tidy sum for this batch.

Carson's trip from his mine was not as secret this time as it had been on previous occasions. A couple of stockmen, Shorty Swink and Milt Holiday, riding after livestock in the vicinity, saw him several different times along the trail as he worked his way down the rough and loggy slope of the West Needle mountains south of Big Molas lake. These men knew Carson quite well but they attached no particular importance to his being in that locality. Later they regretted this oversight. From his location and his course of travel at the point where they first saw him, they knew that he had come from some place farther back in the remote recesses of those rugged and uninviting mountains.

Carson followed his usual ritual in town on this occasion by getting drunk, but he did not go on any extended bender, and he avoided company this time. After celebrating for one day he announced he was pulling out of the mountains for the winter, and that anybody was welcome to follow him that wanted to. No one seemed to want to.

It was late the following autumn before anything more was seen of Carson; then he showed up in Silverton with more rich ore to sell. He did not bring a great deal of it this time. He had not been feeling well that summer, he said, so had not gone to his mine earlier in the season; and when he did go he went direct from his winter quarters, had only stayed there a few days to dig out enough ore for winter expenses. He sold two sacks of his quartz for a tidy sum; and then proceeded to doctor himself as was the custom of the times by getting drunk.

When he left town a couple of days later, he took an ample supply of "medicine" with him in a wooden keg. That evening a couple of men riding across a grassy bench back of the old stage station at Big Molas lake found the old man's body, where it had fallen off the burro he was riding, when he suffered a fatal heart attack. A considerable sum of money was found on his person, along with several specimens of his rich ore; but there was nothing in the form of a map or a description of any kind to indicate the whereabouts of his mine. With his death was lost the actual knowledge of its location.

Before his death Carson had confided to a relative of his that the mine was located somewhere on the northern slopes of the West Needle mountains, but since that district embraces an extensive area of rugged terrain, this bit of general information was not very specific concerning the actual whereabouts of the mine. It was about as useful in a quest for the lost bonanza as the statement that a particular tree grew in a certain big forest would be in a search for that tree. It merely specified the general area.

Carson said the mine was very rich, but had not been extensively developed. It had not been necessary for him to do very much work on the vein to take out his ore; the lead had been fabulously rich in gold from its very outcroppings on the surface, he stated; so all the work he had done had been in "pay dirt." He always left the mine well covered up and completely hidden, he said, whenever he went away. His mine was a long way from his main camp, and was well above timberline. When he worked at the "diggins" he stayed in a sort of crude shelter nearby, made by leaning small poles against an overhanging rock ledge. Everything that he used at the mine had to be transported up there on his own back, he said, because it was inaccessible for packstock.

As the various bits of information about Carson's activities and the probable location of his wonderful mine became pieced together in the years following his death, prospectors and stockmen in the region between Big Molas lake and the West Needles began to look for signs or indications that he might have left which might point to the location of his golden treasure vault.

Some of Carson's old campsites were found in the region. One of these, located in a small basin at timberline on the head of Twilight creek, was the most extensive. This spot was at the northern base of the West Needles, and had been used by Carson as his base camp where he could leave his supplies and extra equipment. The spot afforded excellent pasture for his burros. Across the narrow entrance of the only trail leading into this rock-bound basin Carson had constructed a crude gate to prevent his burros from straying away during his absence.

This whole area was so rough and inaccessible, and so completely covered with dead timber and fallen logs as a result of the big Lime creek burn, that no extensive search was made for Carson's lost bonanza at the time. And since he no longer mysteriously came into Silverton with golden cargoes to stimulate interest in his fabulous mine, concern about its location gradually decreased. No other men seemed to have the hardihood to brave the difficulties and the hardship of that uninviting strip of country that he had possessed. Hunting for his fabulous mine became the topic of conversations around evening campfires, in prospector's cabins, and barrooms where miners assembled. It was easier to hunt treasure under such conditions than it was to get out in the hills and actually look for it. Carson's mysterious mine, however, remained a very live subject in the minds of many of the oldtimers in the district, who, on occasions, related the events associated with it.

Many, many years after Carson's death a stockman's trail was constructed through the rough and loggy area he traveled to Twilight creek, and the Million Dollar highway was built across the Lime creek country between Durango and Silverton. These two thoroughfares opened up the district to travel. Stockmen, prospectors, and fishermen began to prowl over the area.

John Edwards, a professional prospector of Durango, was one of these, and possessed the characteristics of all three classes.

Edwards was a young man in the district at the time of Carson's activities. He knew much of the Carson story at first hand. When the Million Dollar highway was built around Potato mountain and down into the deep Lime creek canyon at the base of the West Needles, it made this spot easy of access and opened up some mighty good fishing. Twilight creek, which drained most of the northern slope of the West Needles, emptied into Big Lime in this locality.

One summer early in the 1920's Edwards combined business and pleasure by pitching his camp on the east bank of Lime creek in a beautiful park there just below the mouth of Twilight. When he was not fishing he went prospecting. His prospecting activities gained the ascendency over fishing after he found a piece of rich "float" on the bank of Twilight creek about a quarter mile east of Lime. This was the same character of ore as Carson's. For years after this discovery, Edwards returned every summer to carry on his search in the vicinity. He always camped on main Lime creek, however, and made his daily prospecting trips from there, and always he went up the drainage of Twilight creek. But he seldom followed that stream to its source on these quests because of the distance through a very rugged terrain. It was too far to go up and back in one day. He was rewarded in his efforts, however, by finding additional bits of float at different spots along the creek, all the way up as far as he went.

On one of his prospecting trips, Edwards found several sticks of dynamite and some short steel drills which he identified as having belonged to Carson. He found these bits of equipment where Carson had left them cached away on a small ledge in a rough and inaccessible side canyon high up on the Twilight drainage, this spot was not far from Carson's base campsite. Edwards figured he was close onto Carson's fabulous discovery when he found this stuff, but after a few futile attempts to find the mysterious vein in the immediate vicinity, he became discouraged. It took energy and effort to follow up the quest in that rugged place, and fishing was much easier. So fishing gained the ascendency in Edwards' activities. Had the lure of the elusive mountain trout been less for Edwards and his energy and his urge for riches been greater, he might have found that golden bonanza that was more elusive than any trout. He surely was not far from it, at that moment, but like many other men he found the quest of treasure trove far easier and more romantic when conducted in imagination and in conversation rather than in the plodding grind of actually hunting it out.

Other men besides Edwards have likewise found rich float in this same vicinity. All of it has been of the same character of quartz and richness as was the Carson ore, and it was all found on Twilight creek. The conclusion that it all came from the same vein, the Carson vein, is inescapable, and that elusive ledge could not be far away. Mike Powell, a stockman of Durango, was one of these other fellows who found a chunk of this same rich ore while he was fishing near the mouth of Twilight creek in August, 1928. This specimen was about the size of a man's fist. It was also a rusty, oxidized quartz thoroughly impregnated with free gold. It assayed thousands of dollars per ton. When Powell found this rock he immediately gave up fishing and went to prospecting in the immediate locality but found no vein or fissure there to encourage him so he gave up the quest. It never occurred to him that this talisman he had picked up came from a golden deposit somewhere several miles away up the mountain slope and had been transported by winter snowslides and other forces of nature to this spot where he picked it up. It could have been "an open sesame" to fortune for him had he followed it to its source.

Juan Quintana, a native Mexican sheepherder, is perhaps the only man other than Carson that ever saw Carson's wonderful mine. And Quintana did not know the importance of his discovery at the time he made it. He accidentally stumbled onto the place, years after Carson's death, while herding sheep in that district. He knew nothing about Carson or about a lost mine in that vicinity when he found those old workings, and he cared nothing about either one. Quintana was a peculiar fellow. He herded sheep by choice, because he preferred solitude and wanted to be left alone, and to be away from human companionship. He did not even want a camp companion. He had no family and few intimate friends. He was cranky, cantankerous, and quarrelsome, but not lazy. To break the monotony of life in the summertime when his flock required very little attention,

84

Quintana would make long hikes over the adjacent country—especially up a mountain slope so he could look over the surrounding country.

In the summer of 1922 Quintana was working for the late J. J. "Jack" McCormick, a sheepman of Durango, Colorado, whose range allotment on the San Juan Forest included the drainage of Twilight creek. In August of that year McCormick established his sheep camp in the little basin at the head of the creek, and only a few feet from the very spot where Carson had set his main camp many years before. McCormick never spent much time in his sheepcamp; when he went out to his outfit he did such work as was necessary there, and then left it alone to his herder for days at a time before he would return again to bring supplies. Such an arrangement as this was exactly to Quintana's liking.

His new camp was at the northern base of the West Needle mountains. Immediately south of him lay the rugged mass of Twilight Peak serrated with innumerable ridges, gulches, bluffs, and benches, and towering several thousand feet above his camp at timberline. This wide expanse of mountainside intrigued Quintana and invited explorations.

On one of his long hikes over these adjacent slopes several days after his camp had been set in Twilight basin, Quintana found a well defined vein of gold ore, some old workings on the vein, and a crude campsite made by poles leaning upright against an overhanging ledge! Remains of an old campfire pit, and a few badly rusted fragments of old tin cans scattered about, gave added evidence of human occupancy of the spot many years before. Shades of Levi Carson! Could this have been his lost bonanza?

This unusual set of conditions aroused Quintana's curiosity. Signs of human occupancy and activity in such an out-of-the-way place merited investigation. Quintana investigated, not with any idea of making a rich strike or discovering a rich mine, but just to satisfy his curiosity. He did not want a mine, would not know what to do with a mine if he had one, and was not hunting for a mine. He was satisfied with his occupation of herding sheep. That was work that he understood and liked, and he had no intentions or desire to change his profession. He had worked in the mines at Telluride one summer several years before but did not like the job, so he had no inclination to find a mine of his own. He did know, however, what it took to make a mine; and he knew what a vein was and what gold looked like in crude ore.

Quintana investigated this extraordinary spot, so concealed in an isolated nook somewhere on the rugged and rocky slopes of the West Needles. He broke several samples from different spots on the vein, and he picked up one fragment of rich ore nearby that had been broken off the vein by someone there many years before. Some of these specimens Quintana threw away on the spot but several of them he put in his pocket and took back to his camp when he returned there with his flock late that evening.

He put three of these specimens, two of the richest he had broken from the vein himself and the old one he had found already broken by someone else, in his duffle bag or "sheepherder's suit case"; the others he laid on top of his "kitchen boxes" in his tent.

Jack McCormick found these samples of ore there when he came to the camp the following afternoon while Quintana was out with the sheep. McCormick looked them over very carefully. They aroused his intense interest. He recognized them as being gold ore of high quality and could easily tell that they had been freshly broken from a vein somewhere. He immediately surmised that Quintana had found a lead somewhere thereabout and had brought these samples from it.

McCormick was a shrewd Irishman who was always on the watch for any way in which he could improve his own fortune, and with a minimum of expense and effort to himself. He figured that here he had a good chance, if he could inveigle Quintana into revealing the location of this vein. His eagerness and his undue solicitude, however, aroused Quintana's suspicions. The Mexican was a peculiar fellow, anyway, and his suspicions were easily aroused.

"I be 'fraid," he confided to a friend long afterwards, "to tell it to Jacky McCormitty anything aboutty de mine. I was 'fraid he kill't me, and keepa de mine. So I no tell't nossin' to him."

In voicing his sentiments in this fashion Quintana was only being natural and was expressing a belief common among the older type of Mexicans of his time that the whiteman would unhesitatingly murder another man over a rich vein in order to eliminate the other fellow and have the mine all to himself.

The harder McCormick tried to elicit information about the location of the vein, the more reticent and taciturn Quintana became, until finally the Mexican got sullen and grouchy and silently went to bed.

McCormick succeeded, however, in persuading Quintana to give him one of the specimens to be assayed. The herder gave him the poorest, leanest one of the lot; and if McCormick had not taken possession of it that night and had not put it in his own pocket immediately, he would have not gotten it at all, because Quintana got up early the following morning, while Jack was still asleep, and took all the remaining specimens out from the camp and buried them under a big spruce tree.

McCormick realized the futility of any further attempts to get information from Quintana at that time, so he left the camp that same day and took his sample of the ore back to Durango to be assayed.

"It was the leanest rock of the lot," McCormick remarked afterwards, "but at that it assayed $500 in gold per ton." And that value was at the old price of gold. It would now be worth $875 per ton.

The high value of the ore stimulated McCormick to make more and greater attempts to get Quintana to show him where the vein was located. He made every reasonable offer that he could think of to entice the Mexican into revealing its whereabouts but to no avail. All the information he could get was that the vein was somewhere in the locality of the camp in Twilight basin, but since that locality embraced quite an extensive area, the task of finding a small outcrop of a vein in it seemed hopeless. Quintana told McCormick nothing about old workings, old campsite, or any other details. He told "Jacky nossin'."

From a safe place of concealment Quintana watched McCormick leave the camp next day and go back down the trail to the Million Dollar highway. The following morning, when the herder was sure that McCormick was gone and that no one else was around in the vicinity, he went back to the place where he had found the vein and the old workings, and very carefully and methodically covered the outcroppings of the vein and the old workings over with rocks and dirt, and he threw the upright poles down from the ledge where they had stood for many years.

"I hide it every ting," he said later, "so nobody can see nossin' dere."

It was not long after this occurrence until Quintana quit working for McCormick. He got tired of being pestered about the location of his discovery. He went to town and, according to his usual custom, went on a bender until all his money was spent. Then he got another job herding sheep on another outfit and dropped out of the picture for several years.

Late in October in 1932, ten years after he had made his remarkable discovery, Quintana got a job herding sheep for another local sheepman, a fellow with whom he had been acquainted for many years. For convenience this man will be called Corny. It was so late in the season by this time that all the sheep outfits had long since left the mountain country, the lambs had been shipped, and the herds, made up for the winter, were on their long trek to the winter ranges. A heavy blanket of snow covered the high country. Quintana's employer was a sheepman of the old school, just as Quintana himself was. The owner himself attended to his camp and looked after his outfit personally. On the drift from the fall range to the winter quarters, the camp was made early each evening, and an old fashioned campfire with its cheerful glow and its warm, friendly atmosphere was an important part of camp life on this outfit. Quintana liked it this way. It revived in him pleasant memories of his youth when the range was free and the days there were happy. He was an old man now, his eyesight was not so good, and he was not the efficient herder he used to be. His new employer, however, was kind and considerate, an attitude which on his part led Quintana into a confidential and communicative mood around the campfire one evening.

On this occasion Quintana narrated the account of his activities and his experiences in connection with his discovery of the rich vein, and in his dealings with McCormck. He told very simply and directly what he had done and why he had done it.

This was the first and the only time Quintana had ever told the story of the part he played in connection with the lost mine. He had never told it to anyone before, he said, because he did not want to be pestered by other people about his discovery. He didn't want to be bothered. He showed Corny the three rich specimens of the ore—the two he had broken from the lead himself and the other one that he had found already broken—and told exactly where he had buried the other pieces of quartz at the base of a tree in Twilight basin to hide them from McCormick. Corny, through long years of experience and of association with men of Quintana's type, understood perfectly the whys and wherefores of such actions and reactions. Years of experience in the school of hard knocks had given him a mighty thorough knowledge of Mexican psychology. With adroit skill he drew the whole story from Quintana, but the Mexican went into so much detail and got his descriptions about the exact location of the vein so muddled in trying to be specific, that it was of little value. Before the evening was over, however, Quintana promised to conduct Corny to the very spot of the rich discovery, the following summer. But for Quintana the following summer never came. He contracted pneumonia that same winter and passed away.

The only living link between the known and the unknown, as far as the Carson mine was concerned, passed out of existence with Quintana's death. Corny, however, considered the fabulous and bountiful reward that could be had, if a man were successful in following Quintana's tangled and involved directions, well worth making an effort, so the following summer he quietly slipped back into Twilight basin to have a try. This was the depression year of 1933 when financial disaster had overtaken stockmen, farmers, bankers, and almost everyone else. Corny had not escaped its adversity. Success in this undertaking would recoup his crippled fortune. But he was a practical man, not a dreamer; many years of experience in the mountains eminently qualified him to appraise the situation properly.

He had no difficulty in finding the big spruce tree where Quintana had cached the samples of ore years before, and he found the several pieces of quartz buried exactly where the Mexican said they would be. They were rich in gold and were of the same character of rock as the three specimens Quintana had shown him

The Baker Brothers' Peculiar Seam in Bedrock

There is just no logical way of accounting for the actions of human beings in hunting for gold. Some men find gold when they are not hunting for it at all; others actually find it in one place while they are merely hunting for another particular spot in which to look for it. And some men find a rich vein "by pecking at a wide seam in the rock for pastime while resting from climbing the mountain"; break enough rich ore from it in a few minutes to exceed a month's wages as a bricklayer, and then walk off and leave the whole project to take a construction job because they are broke and need to "get a job to buy biscuits."

It was just about such a series of incidents as these that happened to the Baker brothers—Sull and Charley—in the San Juan country in southwestern Colorado, late in the summer of the depression year, 1932. The Bakers were sheepmen, not as partners in the business—each brother had a small herd of sheep that he managed independently of the other—but they worked together a great deal and handled their stock on adjacent ranges.

The Bakers lived in Aztec, New Mexico, and wintered their sheep on the semi-desert area in that vicinity. In the summer time, however, in common with the other sheepmen of the region, they drove their herds into the high mountains around the mining town of Silverton, Colorado, for the succulent pasture there. Several small, operating mines and innumerable prospectors were working in the area of the Bakers' summer range, so it was only logical for them to make friends among the mining people and to gain some knowledge of mining and its potentialities. Gold ore was a commodity that would readily convert into cash, and its value was not adversely affected by the depression—two mighty rare qualities in those tough financial times.

Like all other livestock men of that period, the Bakers were having difficult financial "sledding." A long series of drought years in the San Juan country had seriously depleted the open range and had made maximum production in wool and lambs impossible as well as more expensive; and the market price of the product was far below the minimum cost of production. Every sheepman in the region was going broke but could do nothing about it unless he contrived some way of getting an income from some other source. To the Baker brothers mining was an inviting field.

But they were not experienced miners and were hesitant to venture into that activity on their own judgment. They had a good friend, however, by the name of Hendersen, who was an experienced miner, an expert on ores of the Silverton area, and a conservative business man. Hendersen had made a modest fortune in mining in the district and was living in semi-retirement in Silverton at the time. The Baker brothers consulted him about the possibilities of mining and about what would be the best procedure to get into the industry.

"The best thing to do is to find a mine of your own," Hendersen counselled them. "Even if the vein is small, if it is reasonably good pay dirt, you can dig it out yourselves and make a success of the undertaking. It will be better than the sheep business." The Baker brothers, however, were not prospectors, so their next question was how to find a mine. Hendersen had a good, practical suggestion.

Somewhere on the headwaters of West Lime, he said, he did not know the exact spot, was located an abandoned tunnel that had been driven into the mountain on a gold bearing vein by an eccentric old prospector by the name of Flatus. Flatus had died alone in his cabin during the winter time several years previously and nothing further had been done with the property. It was, therefore, open to relocation by anyone who wanted it. Some good ore, he pointed out, had been found in the cabin along with the old man's body. This ore was of excellent commercial quality, if there was sufficient quantity. It would be a good idea to find this tunnel and investigate it. The search for it should not be difficult, because the Bakers would be looking for specific landmarks—the open portal of a tunnel, a mine dump, and a tumbled down cabin—on the surface of the ground instead of hunting for uncertain indications of a vein as would be the case in prospecting for a mine.

The Bakers, especially Sull, were familiar with the West Lime creek section; that area lay immediately west of the Million Dollar highway about twelve to fourteen miles south of Silverton. Every spring Sull drove his flock of sheep along the divide between West Lime and Engine creeks from Engineer Mountain to South Mineral on his way to his summer range at Chattanooga at the foot of Red Mountain pass on the Million Dollar highway above Silverton, while his brother Charley took his herd over the lower driveway across Lime Creek and by Molas Lake. But they both knew the location of that seven-mile strip of mountain territory called West Lime. They decided to have a look.

They were prudent men, however, and determined to do their searching for the Flatus tunnel at convenient times and on a piecemeal basis so as not to interfere with any other profitable undertaking they might find. They had both worked in the building trade before going into the sheep business, and at this time of financial stress they were watching for any opportunities in that field.

In fact their first and most memorable venture into the West Lime area in search of the Flatus tunnel was a sort of byproduct or supplemental excursion in connection with a trip from Silverton to Aztec to see about a building contract on which they had previously submitted a bid. That was only a four-hour drive, so the Bakers figured that by getting an early start from their headquarters at Chattanooga they could spend a goodly part of the day searching along Coal creek, a tributary of Lime, for the tunnel and still get home in good season.

It was shortly after nine o'clock that morning when they pulled off the Million Dollar highway at the familiar Coal creek campground, parked their pickup and camp outfit, and started up the steep canyon on their search for the old Flatus tunnel. Since they were looking for an open hole in the ground, not a lead that might have to be uncovered, they carried no lunch and no tools except a light, prospecting pick. The Bakers were like the great majority of men who have been under similar circumstances—they were looking for a specific thing or set of conditions on this particular mission, went prepared for that one purpose, and gave only minor attention to other occurrences incidental to the trip. They would regret this oversight later.

It was past noontime when the brothers crossed the main fork of Coal creek, high up the mountain slope and not far under the crest of the divide between West Lime and Engine creek. This was familiar ground to Sull because it was adjacent to his sheep driveway, but it was Charley's first visit into the domain. It was beautiful alpine country, so typical of the San Juan mountains high up along the timberline zone. The Bakers were still in the timber, however, but a quarter of a mile farther up the forest abruptly stopped, and the verdant ridge of the high divide extended on in graceful undulations like a green velvet carpet.

The brother climbed up the steep west bank of Coal creek onto the point of land that extended out as a sort of promontory between the main branch of the creek that turned north at this point and went around a timbered ridge into Red Basin, and the west fork which continued directly back into an open basin at the base of Engineer Mountain.

This was a beautiful spot, a triangular bench lying along the bank of West Coal between the stream and the timbered ridge on the north. It was covered with a heavy grassy sod and scattered fir trees—a wonderful camping place. Its marshy slope toward the creek was slight until it reached the edge of the narrow canyon that constituted the water course, here it broke into a steep pitch for a hundred feet or more down to the stream bed itself. Even this precipitous bank was covered with sod except for a few spots here and there, where excessive moisture during rainy seasons, or melting snow during the spring thawing, had caused patches of earth to slip or slide from their natural positions on the shallow underlying bedrock.

There were several of these bare spots along this bank, but the occurrence of such phenomena was so common on steep banks in the mountain country that no one paid much attention to them. They were accepted as a part of the natural geology.

"There is no use in our going any farther up this way," said Sull when he and Charley had climbed up on the brow of the bench. "I have been all over the country above here when I have gone through with my sheep in the spring, and I know there isn't any old mine up that way. I have often hobbled my horses out to pasture on this little flat," indicating the grassy bench with a wave of his hand. "I'm tired from climbing the mountain up to here and I would like to sit down and rest, and have a smoke." And with that remark he pulled his pipe and tobacco can out of the pocket of his jumper and prepared to "have a smoke." It required all the tobacco there was in the can to fill his pipe, and he threw the empty container into a bunch of scrub mountain willows nearby.

"Well, you set down and smoke and rest a bit while I take a turn up the draw and back through the timber on that hillside. I'd like to get a better look at the country above here anyway," said Charley as he set off across the bench toward the head of the canyon.

Sull strolled leisurely along the edge of the little flat where it broke off in the steep pitch to the creekbed, until he encountered a convenient log to sit on. The log lay right on the crest of the precipitous bank. From this position Sull noticed one of these spots where the covering sod had slipped away leaving the bedrock exposed, and cutting diagonally across the upper side of this open space was a "seam" or fissure of a distinctly different character from the adjacent blue-gray, country rock. Sull had seen seams in bedrock before but never anything quite like this one. All the others he had seen had been narrow, had followed a winding course, and had never protruded much above the base rock.

This one, however, was eight or ten inches wide, protruded a couple of inches above the bedrock, was of a very different color and texture, and it followed a straight course. The extraordinary conditions aroused Sull's curiosity. Such a freak seam deserved investigation, and investigating it would help to pass the time until Charley returned. He knocked the ashes out of his pipe, put it in his pocket, and slid down the grassy bank onto the bare spot and, with his prospector's pick, began to break pieces off from the seam.

The rock was hard and brittle but it broke easily and with sharp cleavages. Sull was farsighted and had difficulty in distinguishing details at close range without his glasses, and in

95

roughing around on the range he got along well enough, he said, so that he never had his "reading glasses" with him. He could see well enough, however, to distinguish that rock he was breaking from the "seam" was a rusty, brown color and was thoroughly impregnated with small particles of bright metal. It never occurred to him that it might be gold, or that the "seam" might be a vein.

He was not hunting for either one of these things on this trip. He and Charley were looking for an abandoned tunnel—and certainly this freak seam was no tunnel.

Sull continued, however, to break fragments from the streak, to look at each one and then lay it down on the pile that he was accumulating on the bedrock. Some of the pieces he broke off were "as big and as thick as a man's hand but they broke to a feather edge on the lower side." He became so absorbed in his unusual pastime that he did not hear Charley approach to the edge of the bank above him.

"Well, where is the mine?" jokingly asked Charley.

"Right here," humorously replied Sull. "I've found it and already got our fortune mined out. Look at this rock and tell me what you think of it," and with that remark he tossed a couple of the freshly broken fragments up to Charley.

"It sure has a different color from the rest of the rocks around here, and it's got a lot of metal of some kind in it," responded Charley after a rather casual inspection of the samples. "But come on, and let's get on down to camp and get some dinner. I'm getting hungry, and it is getting late. And we better be getting down country to see about that job. We can look at these samples later."

"Coming up, just as soon as I can put a handful of this 'ore' in my pocket," replied Sull as he stuffed several pieces of the freshly broken fragments into the pocket of his jumper.

On their return trip down the canyon to their camp, the Bakers held a course close to the stream bed. A short distance below the mouth of Coal creek, and not far from the point of discovery of the "seam," they encountered a high ledge of rock over which the waters of the creek cascaded in a waterfall of several feet, but the brothers could not descend over the bluff at that point. They had to backtrack a short distance and take a circuitous route around the end of the ledge in order to continue their journey.

After they had gotten back to their truck, had gotten their campfire going, and had their dinner under way, they again looked at the samples of rock.

"Let's drop one in the fire and roast it," suggested Sull, "and we can get it out of the ashes and look at it before we leave. If that metal in it is gold, it will be sticking out in bubbles by that time and will be easy to distinguish." So Sull dropped a good-sized specimen into the glowing embers.

But they became so absorbed in getting their camp packed back into the truck and in getting on their way to see about the prospective building contract that they forgot all about the fragment of rock in the fire until they were many miles down the road toward Durango. They figured it was too far back by that time for them to return for it, and besides, it was not, they thought, of much importance anyway. The important thing was to get on down to Aztec and get the building job which would mean at least a little tangible income in that time of financial stress.

It is odd how some of the little things of life sometimes unconsciously influence men in making momentous decisions, and how some things that seem so insignificant at the time will later prove to be highly important while the important thing of the moment later proves to be so inconsequential, so trivial.

When the Bakers got home that night, Sull hung his jumper, with the fragments still in its pocket, up in his workshop where it remained until the following midwinter. Charley put the two specimens Sull had tossed to him away in a cigar box with other trinkets. And both men promptly forgot all about their specimens.

In fact the way things worked out for them, they were too busy the balance of that summer and autumn to give any further attention to mining or prospecting of any sort. They got the contract for building a house for a neighbor in Aztec, so between that construction job and looking after their little sheep outfits they were extremely busy until late in January, 1933, when the building job was completed.

Their interest in their "find" was renewed, however, one day that winter when Sull removed his jacket from the nail where he had hung it the past August when he had returned from their trip up Coal Creek. The weight of the ore samples, still in the pocket where he had put them the day he broke them from the "seam," refreshed his memory. He removed them from the pocket of the jacket and examined them more closely with his "reading glasses" on this time. He was convinced that the metal in them was native gold. Charley, however, was not so certain.

In order to settle their argument, and to satisfy their curiosity, they concluded to take some of the samples and show them to their old mining friend, Hendersen, who was spending the winter in Durango.

Hendersen immediately recognized the samples as being a brown, sugar quartz typical of the freegold bearing ores of the Silverton district. The fragments were rich in gold, he said, mighty rich. Hendersen's verdict could be summed up in his own words: "If you fellows have as much as fifty pounds of that ore, you are financially well fixed."

"Oh, we got that much mined out already," replied Sull.

"Where?" inquired Hendersen.

"Up on Coal creek," Sull said.

"On Coal creek," repeated the old man almost incredulously. "Man, you must have found what is thought to be one of the richest veins in the Silverton district. Considerable rich 'float' has been found along Coal creek in years gone by, and mining men of the region are convinced that a mighty rich lode crosses that section somewhere. That vein has been diligently hunted for by lots of good prospectors. Can you go back to the place where you found it?"

"I sure can," replied Sull. "I know that country like a book. I could go back there with my eyes shut."

"Don't need to do that," said Hendersen, "better go back with both eyes open this time. I'll go with you fellows if you want me to and give you my opinion of it."

The Bakers were glad to have Hendersen volunteer to accompany them and to have the benefit of his mining experience and his practical judgment. Accordingly it was agreed that the three of them would go up to look at the vein just as early in the spring as snow conditions would permit. The date could not come too soon for the Bakers, because they properly figured their financial difficulties would be eliminated with that initial trip. Added strength was given to their convictions a few days later when returns came from an assay, made at the old man's suggestion. It was worth $44,000 per ton! A bonanza! (And that value was still at the old price of gold. The following March the value of gold was increased 75% by presidential decree, thereby adding $33,000 in value to each ton of the ore.)

Small wonder that the Bakers were anxious to return to their vein. Sull estimated he had broken off at least $500 worth of the ore when he found the "seam," and had carelessly left the fragments piled on the bedrock by the vein. He figured all he had to do was to take a sack up the mountain with him on his return, walk over to the bare spot on the steep bank, and scoop $500 worth of gold ore into his bag. It was just as simple as that. It was a mighty pleasant outlook during a gloomy winter and dreary financial times!

The snow fall in the San Juan country was extra heavy during the winter of 1932-33. It piled deep in the high country, and big banks of it along the ridges and in sheltered spots were slow in melting. It was early in July before the Bakers and their mining friend Hendersen figured they could make a successful trip up Coal creek to the vein. The Bakers in anxious impatience had made one exploratory excursion earlier that spring to keep a check on snow conditions in the region and to be sure the area would be open when they took Hendersen up there.

On this trip of inspection they parked their pickup in the same place they had camped the previous summer when Sull found the "seam" and had dropped the fragment of rock into the campfire. They remembered the incident this time and promptly went over to their old fire bed to examine the roasted bit of rock they had so completely forgotten at that time. The fire bed had not been disturbed in the meantime. It was just as they had left it and Sull remembered the exact spot in the ashes where he had put the specimen of ore. He had already put on his "reading glasses" in order to see the specimen better as soon as he could pick it from the old fire pit.

"Holy Smoke and Sam Hill," ejaculated Sull using his favorite expletive, with his first look at the roasted fragment of rock. "This rock is plumb lousey with gold. There are gold bubbles sticking out all over it. Take a look at it." And he handed it to Charley.

"Oh boy!" exclaimed Charley. "It's got a lot on it. Too bad we forgot to look at this last summer. Ain't it?"

"Sure is. Had we looked at it then we'd gone right back up the mountain and got the rest of it that I had broken off."

"Ah well, it hasn't spoiled over the winter, and it is worth more now than it was then, and we can get it just as well now, as soon as we can get up there," philosophically remarked Charley.

Visual education is a great thing. The fact that the Bakers were able actually to see so much gold in the specimen was far more impressive on them than big figures on an assay sheet. It stimulated their eagerness to get back to their discovery, and to gather up the pile of broken ore of which this fragment had been a part. The snow conditions of course on this particular trip prevented them from getting all the way up to the spot, but put no damper on their enthusiasm.

Two or three weeks later when the three men—the Baker brothers and their older friend Hendersen—set out to rediscover and "appraise" the vein, Sull could not restrain his eagerness and hold himself down to the slower pace of his companions. He was tall and slender but muscular, rather impulsive, and full of energy, and in spite of his 50-odd years, he could climb around over the mountains like a goat. Charley was a few years younger. He was short and stout and more reserved and quiet than Sull. Hendersen was a rather frail old man in his seventies. The pace up the mountain had to be set to suit Hendersen's abilities. About half way up the canyon, Sull remarked to his two companions: "You fellows are too slow for me. I'm going ahead on up to the 'mine,' and begin to dig out some gold. I'll see you up there." And with that remark he was off.

On his way up the canyon he noted several different landmarks he and Charley had seen the preceding summer. At the proper point on the streambed he began his detour around the bluff where the waterfall was, and where he and Charley had had to backtrack at that time. He crossed the creek above the falls and ascended the familiar east slope of the bench where he had climbed it the past August, and walked rapidly, eagerly across the grassy flat on top to the spot where he thought Charley stood when he caught the two fragments of ore Sull had tossed him at that time. From this point Sull fully expected to see the familiar open spot of bedrock, with its transversing vein and pile of broken ore by it, on the steep bank of West Coal creek. But when he looked over the edge of the bank neither the spot nor any of the objects on it were there! Sull was so amazed at this unexpected situation that it took several minutes for him to grasp the magnitude of the disappointment. This just had to be the place although the steep bank didn't look the same as he had remembered it from the summer before. It seemed there was something subtly different about it—something he could not figure out; but this was unmistakably the proper bank because there was the grassy bench about which there could be no doubt or confusion.

He had just come up to the wrong point, he reasoned. Funny how his judgment could get so confused. Such a thing had never happened to him before. He knew the exposed spot of bedrock with the transversing vein was on that bank. He'd find it by scouting around a bit. He looked for the log he had sat on at that time, but no log was there! He scouted along the edge of the bench for a quarter mile or more to its upper end—a point far beyond where he knew he had traveled the year before—but he found no proper spot of bedrock, no log, no vein. He was, to use his own expression, "completely bumfuzzled."

In the meantime, as Sull was returning from the upper end of the bench, Charley and Hendersen came up onto the east end of it at about the same point Sull had, and Charley had walked straight across the grassy flat to the same point on the bank as Sull had done and had expected to see the open bedrock, the vein, and the pile of ore (and Sull breaking more).

Charley was similarly "bumfuzzled." Hendersen of course had never been there before.

"Where is the mine and all that ore?" Charley called out to Sull as the latter approached.

"Hanged if I know," responded Sull. "I thought the blamed

thing was right here" indicating by gesture an area of the steep bank immediately below them.

"So did I. And I expected to find you down there loading ore into your sack when we got here."

"I was afraid something like this would happen," remarked Hendersen. "You fellows are not the first men to find a vein and then not be able to go to it later. It has happened a lot of times before. In some way or another you have got your locations confused."

"Maybe we got the exact spot confused, but not the general location. That vein has got to be around here someplace. We will find it yet."

Sull and Charley reviewed the incidents that had occurred there the previous summer when Sull had found the open spot of bedrock and the vein; and they agreed that according to their recollections the spot should be somewhere in the immediate vicinity of where they were then standing, but since it was not, they both must be at some fault in their memories and that the particular spot must be somewhere else in that immediate area. They began a careful search round about. They found the empty tobacco can Sull had thrown away the preceding summer, but that was the only tangible thing they found that furnished any clue, and that one proved to be useless. How far Sull had gone after discarding the can they could not figure out, nor could they find a log of any sort that could possibly be the unstable landmark Sull sat on at that time. An occasional log lay on the creek bed at the foot of the bank, but the one they were searching for had been on the crest at the top of the bank.

"The more we hunted the more bumfuzzled we got," said Sull afterwards, "until finally we got so disgusted that we gave up for that day." But by no means had they given up completely. They made several return trips during the following four years in quest of their lost bonanza, always hoping on each trip that some fortunate something would occur to help them solve the mystery and to enable them again to find the "peculiar seam" that could be their open sesame to riches. And they consistently kept their mouths tightly closed and guarded their secret well. They made no attempt to cash in on it with anyone or to promote a "grub-stake" on the strength of it.

The Baker brothers did just what any other normal, reliable man would have done under the same circumstances. They figured they had a good thing and they did not want to be dividing it up with someone else. If some other fellow could rediscover the spot, they could too; so they kept silent and kept trying.

But the discovery of gold in a mining district is something that just cannot be kept a complete secret. In one way or another bits of the information will get out, and then rumor takes over to fill in the gaps and a story gets underway. And so it was with the Bakers, and in the spring of 1938 they related the account of their discovery to the writer and enlisted his help in the search. The writer was glad to participate, and here is why:

As a rangeman I had worked all over the Lime creek area, and as a miner I had worked in many different mines in the San Juan country. I was familiar with ores and the formations in which they occurred, and with the tremendous potentialities of a rich gold vein in virgin ground. I was particularly interested in the Coal creek drainage because I knew about a few pieces of rich float that had previously been found along that streambed. I was positive there was a rich, undiscovered vein up there somewhere.

I was so sure of it that in the summer of 1930 I put up a short grubstake for Nat Nelson, an experienced miner friend of mine, to prospect on Coal creek for a couple of weeks. Nelson was a thorough and painstaking prospector, but prospecting is slow business when it is done right. Nelson found two pieces of float of extremely rich gold ore at two different points on Coal creek above the Million Dollar highway; but he did not have time to pursue his quest any further then. The ore he found was a brown, rusty quartz filled with free gold—the kind of ore so typical of the Lime creek section.

Then, in the summer of 1933 while I was working on the Golden Eagle mine at the head of West Lime, I slipped down to Coal creek one Sunday in early September to prospect. At the time, I knew nothing about the Baker brothers' strike there. It was a dry fall and Coal creek had only a small stream of water, which was a condition favorable to my task. I wanted to work

103

the streambed for "float" to guide me to the vicinity of the vein which would necessarily be somewhere higher up on the structure. I went up Coal creek to a point above the rotted abutments of the bridge on the old toll road where Nelson had showed me he found the last piece of float in 1930, and began my prospecting there. A couple of hundred yards up stream I found a bit of the rich, brown quartz, not bigger than the end of a man's thumb, but it was the real thing. It gave me a big thrill because it was the first float I personally had found on Coal creek, and it was positive proof of the existence of a rich lead not too far away. I got overly anxious and too impatient with the slow progress I was making up the creek in my time-consuming, careful investigation of each small gravel bar for more float, so I pushed along quite rapidly until I encountered a high bluff across the streambed where there was a waterfall about 20 feet high. I could go no farther up the stream without making a detour. This was the same ledge around which the Bakers detoured the previous year.

Above the water line on the edge of the small basin made by this waterfall at the base of the ledge, I saw a fragment of rock which I judged was a piece of quartz. It was a rusty color, of irregular shape, and only partially covered with sand and silt. I picked it up, and, Holy Smoke! it was quartz—*the quartz*—chock-full of gold!

It was an irregular shaped piece of rock a couple of inches wide by about three inches long. One side of it was as thick as a man's hand at the base of the thumb, and it tapered to a sharp feather-edge on the other side. Its cleavages were sharp and rough, and its broken side was not badly oxidized, indicating it had been broken from the vein in the recent past. Its sharp edges and rough cleavages proved it had not come far and had not been exposed to the grinding, polishing forces of erosion very long. Its shape showed it had been broken off from the lead by a violent blow rather than by the slower processes of nature—possibly a loose stone rolling down the mountainside had struck an exposed spot on the vein and had knocked off this large chip in recent years. To me it was an urgent invitation to do further prospecting in the area, but it was too late to do so that day. I looked forward to coming back the next Sunday, but I didn't make it.

The Lucky Discovery Mining Company, which was then operating the Golden Eagle property, made a deal for the old Lucky Moon mine in the La Plata mountains, and I was one of the crew transferred to that operation, more than 100 miles distant.

However, I kept my choice piece of float, remembered where I found it, and always dreamed of getting back to renew my prospecting for the vein in that area; and like the Bakers and other men under similar circumstances, I kept my mouth shut about my "find." That was my secret and I kept it.

But as time passes and other pressing activities crowd into a man's attentions in the fierce struggle to make a living, the importance of events that have gone before seems to fade somewhat, and the initial ambition and enthusiasm for a past project gradually diminishes until, oftentimes, it becomes but a pleasant dream; and so it was with me in getting back to prospect on Coal creek, until the Bakers related their experiences to me in 1938. This was six years after their original discovery in the area, and five years after mine. A lot of natural changes can happen in a given terrain in that length of time, and a person can forget innumerable details of the topography and the relative positions of various landmarks. It is easy then to get confused.

But my enthusiasm was rekindled by my conversation with the Bakers. It seemed unmistakable that Sull had found the vein I was hunting for. The facts seemed to prove that the fragment of rich ore I had found at the base of the waterfall was one Sull had chipped from the vein in 1932. It was the same ore, and he distinctly remembered breaking fragments of that shape at that time, but of course he did not remember that particular piece. My sample assayed $36,000 as against $44,000 in the previous one from the specimens Sull had taken, but this discrepancy was no serious matter. We were convinced that my sample came from the same pile as his did. The winter snows had pushed it down the steep bank to the streambed where it got frozen in a bit of ice which was carried down stream in the spring freshets, went over the waterfall, and lodged on the edge of the basin where I found it.

Until our conversation neither the Baker brothers nor I knew anything about what each of us had done on Coal creek. We pooled our knowledge and it looked like a mighty good bet that we would find the elusive bonanza—but we didn't. So far as I am concerned it is still as elusive as ever.

I had no difficulty in going back to the place where I found my specimen, that spot was unmistakable, but the small basin was so altered by an excessive amount of debris that had I been looking for a particular rock I had seen there previously I would never have found it.

We went on up stream to the grassy bench and the steep bank bordering it that Sull remembered so well. We had no trouble finding those, but there our smooth sailing ended.

Details on the surface of the ground had changed the appearance of the place in many minor ways: small trees that had attracted no attention when Sull made his discovery had grown to be sizeable saplings in spots where Sull would have sworn no trees existed; an open spot of exposed bedrock on the steep bank where Sull was sure no spot had been before and grassy sod over some other spot where he though the bedrock should be bare; and the grassy bench seemed to encroach over the crest of the steep bank—making a more pronounced brow on the crest of the precipitous incline. These various factors all helped to confuse him about distances involved in the events that happened on that memorable day in August, 1932. It was all very discouraging.

I had no doubt about Sull's having found a vein somewhere on that steep bank, but so far as any specific information we could develop, he might have found it anywhere in an area several hundred feet long and forty to fifty feet wide and all covered with an overburden from a few inches to ten feet deep. To undertake the removal of so much earth with pick and shovel was too big a job.

However, as nature uncovered the vein one time and then covered it over again, so she will repeat the process sometime in the future. The grassy sod that makes the verdant covering on the shallow bedrock of the bench and the steep bank broke away to expose the vein that Sull found, and then slipped again, like a rug on a hard, smooth floor, to recover it again. So the same sort of natural phenomenon will be repeated in the future when natural conditions are proper to bring such a change about.

Fortunate will be the person that passes by there then to find that "peculiar seam in bedrock" openly inviting him through a golden door to riches.

I am going to try to be that lucky guy.

The Golden Fortune on Timber Hill

The mere possession of gold does not make men rich. The precious yellow metal, to be effective in accomplishing its coveted magic, must be gotten from its secret vaults in nature into the artificial vaults of commerce before its commanding power can really be utilized. Gold, buried in the mountain, whether in its natural state or cached away as bullion, is not money in the bank. And to get gold from the mountain to the bank is not always easy, as Buster Reede and "Soapy" Robinson found out in the San Juan country of southwestern Colorado in the early days of mining in that region.

Their hard experiences laid the foundation for many other men to try unsuccessfully to accomplish this same difficult task with the same heavy bars of gold bullion that Reede and Soapy failed with. Not all the men making the attempt were failures, however, and the two who did finally succeed did the job easily and in a short time. But that is the way the "breaks" go in the fascinating, the alluring, occupation of hunting lost treasure.

Buster Reede and Soapy Robinson were an odd pair, working under conditions that were strange to them, and their reactions to incidents that happened during the few months that they were in the mining country were a strange mixture of contradictions.

Buster Reede was a clean-cut, young man, about thirty years old, stout, stocky, and straightforward in speech and action. He had been raised on a midwestern farm, but in his late twenties he had drifted West in search of fortune and adventure just as many other youths of the period had done.

In his many and varied jobs in machine shops, sawmills, and steamplants, since leaving the farm, Reede had acquired a good working knowledge of machinery before he teamed up with Soapy Robinson to seek fortune in the booming mining district of the San Juan mountains in southwestern Colorado.

Soapy Robinson was a tall, slender man, an untidy individual with dark hair, dark whiskers tinged with gray, and shifty, dark eyes that were constantly watching for any opportunity to benefit Soapy, whether that opportunity was honest or not—hence his sobriquet of "Soapy" because he was so slick in his conduct. He was past sixty and was said to have served a long term in a midwestern penitentiary for an armed robbery in which murder was committed. He was then out on parole.

It was in the spring, circa 1883, that the two men, outfitted with three burros, food, camp equipment, and mining tools, started out for the mining country. The main route into the San Juan mountains at that time was up the Rio Grande from Del Norte and over the high crest of the Continental Divide via Timber Hill and the famous, rockbound Stony Pass and down the Animas drainage to Silverton—the "rough and tumble" frontier town that was the hub of activities of the region.

Reede and Soapy did not stay long in the Silverton area, however. Several rich strikes around Ophir on the South Fork of the San Miguel river led them to travel on over to that district to seek their fortune. They found that section to be a mighty lively place.

In the excitement caused by the recent rich discoveries, miners and prospectors were scattered all over the area with mining claims staked and cross staked everywhere, and a steady stream of rich golden ore poured into the smelting plant presumably of The Boston and Ophir Smelting Company, which was then in its second year of operation.

The mining excitement, with its alluring prospects to men of making a rich discovery, made it difficult for the smelter management to get and to keep efficient help; and Buster Reede found the confusion of prospecting for a vein and an open spot on which to locate a claim entirely too frustrating for him. To him the prospect of a steady job at the smelter at the marvelous wages of $3.50 per day for a ten-hour shift was far more attractive. With his knowledge of machinery and his past experiences in machine work of various kinds, he had no difficulty in obtaining employment at the plant.

"I tell you what, Buster," said Soapy, "we'll set our camp over on that little flat close to the smelter, and I'll do the cookin' and prospect on the side while you are workin', and mebbe we ken make sumpin' out o' this deal yit."

Reede got along well in his work at the smelter. By the end of his first month there he had learned the why and the wherefore of all the processes and of all the machinery used in the reduction of the crude ores and the refining of the gold in the big roasters into bars of bullion which weighed 40 pounds and were worth $12,800 each (at the old price of gold). At that time Ophir was thirty-five mountain miles from the nearest railhead at Silverton, Colorado. The trip across country had to be made with pack animals, so the smelting company stored the bars of bullion in its laboratory at the plant until it had accumulated a sufficient number to send by guarded pack train to Silverton. The capacity of the smelter was sixty tons of crude ore per day, so the bars of bullion accumulated pretty fast; by early autumn the first small shipment was made from the plant, and the accumulating of a second one was immediately begun.

In the meantime Soapy Robinson had tended the camp, had done some prospecting on the side, and had picked up a lot of information about "high grading" and other sharp tricks of an early day mining camp. He and Reede had often discussed the refining processes at the smelter and the storage of gold bullion there.

"Yu' know, Buster, a few of those gold bricks would be a mighty rich haul if we could jest figger out a way to get 'em out uv that labertory without gettin' caught. We cud make a nice little stake easy and mighty quick thataway."

The idea intrigued Reede. He was no saint; and since time immemorial in the mining camps of the West the act of "high grading" has never been considered a low or a dishonorable crime among miners themselves, although it was a criminal offense for which the perpetrators could be sent to prison. The dishonorable part was in getting caught.

As the second shipment of gold bars continued to accumulate at the smelter, Reede and Soapy kept laying their plans and watching for an opportunity to carry them out. Their plan was a bold but simple one. Reede would continue to work at the plant and would watch for a chance to slip a few bars of bullion out of the building without being detected, and by a prearranged signal he would notify his partner Soapy who kept a constant watch from the camp and would be ready to sneak up to the smelter and get the bullion away from there promptly.

Time slipped by, however, with no opportunity for Reede to raid the treasure storage. Indian summer had passed and a misty haze hung in the air denoting an approaching snowstorm in the high country. Reede and Soapy did not want to be snowed in the mountains for the winter, and they had two high passes, Ophir and Stony, to cross on their way out of the mountains. It was the last day of October, pay day at the smelter, and Reede had given the management notice that he would quit at the end of his shift that night.

Reede and Soapy both had about given up hope of carrying out their plan to acquire sudden wealth when a lucky break came their way in the closing period of Reede's last shift at the plant. The other workmen went to the boardinghouse for a midnight lunch and left Reede alone at the smelter. The laboratory where the bullion was stored was, of course, locked, but that condition was no great obstacle to Reede. He picked the lock and hastily dropped five bars of bullion out through a window he opened on the backside of the room. He closed the window, went out through the door and locked it again behind him, slipped out by the side of the smelter and signaled Soapy of his success and was quietly attending to his duties when the other workmen returned. Reede did not hurry to leave the plant immediately after the other men got back from lunch although his shift ended at midnight. He lingered for a time as though he was reluctant to leave. Such was far from the truth, however. It would be hard for any man to be calm with $64,000 in gold bullion lying loose and unguarded on the ground outside. He remained in the plant to keep watch on the other men and to give Soapy time to get the bullion away from the plant. He was not worried that his act would be discovered by the men on the inside of the building because he knew that none of them had access to the storageroom. Only the assayer had a key and he would not come on duty until eight o'clock in the morning, and then he might or might not miss the bars of bullion immediately. Reede had been careful not to dis-

111

turb any of the equipment in the laboratory so as not to arouse the assayer's suspicions immediately upon coming to work.

Reede's artificial attitude of calmness completely disappeared as soon as he had gone a few steps into the hazy moonlight outside the smelter building. He increased his pace of travel, as fast as was consistent with caution, toward his own camp to ascertain if Soapy had seen his signal and had been successful in finding and removing those precious bars of bullion.

He had gone a scant hundred yards when he saw, in the misty gloom, what he thought was the form of a man scrooched down to appear as a small bush.

"Is that you, Soapy?" he asked in a low tone.

"Yep. It's me. I didn't know whether it was you or somebody else comin' so I tried to get down out o' sight."

"Didja see my signal?"

"I shore did, and I come just as fast as I cud."

"Didya find the bullion?"

"Yeah, five bars of it. How many didja throw out?"

"Five. Where are they?"

"Two of 'em are down to camp already, and I got the other three here. Gimme a hand with 'em and let's get to hell out of here while the goin' is good."

And get to hell out of there they did in very short order. Soapy had the burros tethered out near the camp; and while he brought them in and saddled them, Reede got the packs ready to be loaded. Time was of the essence in successfully escaping with their valuable treasure. The quicker they got away, and the farther they traveled before the loss of the bullion was discovered at the smelter, the greater would be their chances of ultimate success.

The camp outfit and supplies plus the additional weight of 200 pounds of gold bullion made each burro's load pretty heavy, but none of the stuff could be discarded because the men needed all of it for the long trip through the mountains before they could reach any place to replenish their supplies.

In his scouting around in the district during the summer, Soapy had become familiar with all the trails in the vicinity, so he and Reede had no difficulty, even in the hazy moonlight, finding their way to the main trail over Ophir Pass. They pushed their heavily loaded burros along as fast as they dared to, and avoided meeting anyone if they possibly could, so as to make it more difficult for anyone who might pursue them.

They skirted around the town of Silverton and followed the old freight road up Cunningham Gulch and over Stony Pass onto the Rio Grande watershed. So far good luck had been with them and they had plenty of reasons to believe they were going to make a clean get away with their tidy fortune.

It was late afternoon of that early November day when they crossed the Continental Divide and began the long zigzag descent of the old road down Grassy Hill to the floor of the canyon. The sky was overcast with murky clouds and an awesome silence pervaded the mountains, both of which factors indicated an approaching heavy snowstorm—not a nice thing in which to get caught deep in the Rockies so late in the fall. Reede and Soapy pressed their tired burros along as fast as they could hoping that they might make it past the old feed station at the foot of Grassy, and then on down to the foot of Timber Hill to camp that night.

It was beginning to get dark when they passed the mouth of Bear Creek where it emptied into the Rio Grande and started down through the timber on the long, rocky grade known as Timber Hill—a famous section of the old freight road from the Rio Grande to Silverton.

About half way down the hill one of their burros became exhausted and would travel no farther. It was well after dark then, so the men decided to camp there by the side of the trail and let the jacks have a night's rest. It was a good camping spot on a little flat at the north base of a timbered knob with a little creek running parallel to the trail and about sixty feet from the base of the hill. Up the creek a little way was a small, open, grassy park where the pack animals could be hobbled out for the night. So far, so good, their luck had held, and they now felt quite confident of getting out of the mountains without getting caught with their bountiful fortune. They figured that the magnificent sum of $64,000 in gold was a very generous reward for one summer spent in the mountains. They felt like rich men, and who wouldn't, with that much money in 1883?

113

About daylight the next morning a few light snowflakes began to fall. The storm that had been threatening for several days had begun. And Reede and Soapy had at least fifty miles yet to travel before they could be reasonably safe from getting snowbound. They had no time to lose. Reede went after the burros while Soapy got breakfast, but he found only two of the jacks alive; the other one, the one that had fagged out the evening before, was dead.

The loss of the one pack animal complicated matters, and the fact that the snow was steadily falling by this time, indicating that a real winter storm was on, added to the difficulties.

Soapy sized up the situation when he said to Reede: "There ain't but one thing to do, and that's to cache four of them gold bars somewhar around here whar we kin find 'em agin in the spring. Load the rest of the stuff on the jacks and git outta here afore we git snowed in."

That seemed to be the only practical solution of their difficulties, so they set about getting the job done. They buried the gold and took note of the natural landmarks about the spot, so they would be sure to recognize it when they returned to get the bullion. There would be no chance of missing the place because this was the only trail, at that time, between the Rio Grande and Stony Pass, and this particular spot was the only way the trail could go through this specific strip of territory. So, insofar as Reede and Soapy were concerned, their problem was to note landmarks well enough in their minds so they would make no mistake in recognizing exactly this spot again in the spring. There was the steep, timbered knob, with outcroppings of rock ledges at irregular intervals up the slope of it to the top, and across the little creek to the north was a high mountain side with scattered timber around a big patch of "slide rock." Immediately across the creek north of their camp was a small open spot, surrounded with mountain willows, and with three big rocks in it. Below this spot was a grove of quaken aspen saplings, and just above, or west of it, a lone spruce tree stood on the bank of the stream near a low protruding point of rock. But to mark the spot more certainly, Reede cut a big blaze of rather peculiar shape on a spruce tree right by the side of the trail where the camp was, and across

114

the stream he took his axe and cut blazes on the east or "down-side" of 15 or 20 of the aspen saplings, so the markings could be easily seen by anyone coming up the trail from the Rio Grande; then he went to the lone spruce tree and marked it by cutting the ends off from several of its lower branches on the north side of the trunk. But there was no definite pattern in these markings, to indicate the precise spot where the gold was buried. This being done, they carried the pack saddle of the dead burro up the side of the timbered knob and hid it among the branches of a big spruce tree there.

Then with two burros packed with their camp outfit, food, and one bar of gold bullion, they set out down the trail for civilization and home.

They got to Pueblo, Colorado, in the course of several days and cashed the one bar of bullion they had been able to take with them. They had no difficulty in selling their gold because in those days the laws governing the sale of gold were not so strict. No questions were asked and a man was not required under the law to disclose where his gold had come from. Disposition of high grade in those days was easy, which might justify a gold miner in these later years to refer to that period as being "the good old days."

But something happened that winter. Soapy Robinson was somewhat of a wild character at best, and it is reported that he was killed in a shooting scrape. Reede, on the other hand, was a conservative sort of chap. He invested his money in a stock farm somewhere in the middle west, and was too busy in the spring to return by himself to retrieve the cache. He figured it was safe anyway where it was and he could come back and get it any time he needed it; and his own personal risk of getting caught by the smelting company would be far less if he waited a year or two before coming back after it by himself. Not another living person knew anything about the cache, so he knew that no one would be hunting for it, and he had hidden it so well he was confident that no one would just stumble on to it by accident.

In the meantime he got married, prospered in his business, and began to raise a family. Always he was busy and interested in his activities and the long hard trip back into the Rockies seemed a tough one to make, and it was so easy to postpone it from year to year. He was never hard-pressed for finances, so he never really needed the gold he had cached away; and as time slipped by it dulled the memory of the cache, mitigated the active interest in it and relegated it into a sort of future treasure hunt that was pleasant to dream about. And so the years slipped by until 1926, more than forty years from the time the cache was made. Reede was an old man then, almost 70; and in the meantime advancing civilization had made many changes in the San Juan country. In September of that year Reede came to Colorado on his vacation in quest of his buried treasure. On this trip, however, he came in his automobile, not with pack burros. All along the Rio Grande valley above Creede he saw big stock farms, fences, big homes and stores where the country had been open and unsettled when he passed through there so many years before. The thing that baffled him the most, however, was that far back in the mountains almost where the long climb up to Stony Pass should begin, he found a big dam across the Rio Grande and instead of a wide, grassy valley with the old freight road winding through it he discovered a huge lake—The Farmers' Union Reservoir.

This immense artificial body of water so altered the topography of the area that Reede became completely confused. He camped near the lake and scouted around there several days trying to solve the riddle. The few people he encountered around the lake were tourists or comparative newcomers who knew nothing about the old freight road to Silverton, or any of the landmarks of the early days. They could not give him any information that was of any help. Time was running out on the old man. He had never before told the story of his golden cache to anyone in the San Juan country, but now he decided to do so in order to obtain definite information for himself about the location of the old trail and the place where he had hidden his treasure. His earlier trip through this section had been so hurried that he had not learned the names of the minor landmarks like Timber Hill or Grassy. The prominent ones, like Rio Grande and Stony Pass, he did know.

Shortly after noon on the last day of his vacation near the upper end of the Farmers' Union Reservoir Reede met Levi Brinkerhoff, a professional packer with a string of pack mules from Silverton.

Brinkerhoff had just brought a party of sportsmen with all of their gear over from Silverton to spend a few days in an outing at the lake, and was then on his return trip back to headquarters in the mining town.

Reede narrated his story very briefly to Brinkerhoff but gave a detailed description about the spot and the markings at the place where he and Soapy had camped and had hidden the gold bullion so many years before. He asked Brinkerhoff if he could give any clue as to where that spot was located or how to find the way to it.

"If I can find those markings," said Reede, "I'll know exactly where to dig for the bullion; and I won't have to dig deep."

"I have never noticed the particular markings you have mentioned," said Brinkerhoff. "There are so many markings along the old trail that I never paid special attention to any of them, but the place you are hunting for must be up on Timber Hill. I'm going up by there now. If you want to come along, I'll show you the trail."

"How far is it from here?"

"About eight or nine miles."

"I haven't time to go up there and get back this afternoon, and I got some folks waiting for me down at my camp, but I'll make the trip tomorrow."

But Reede did not make that trip to Timber Hill. That evening a messenger came to his camp with an important message urging his immediate return home. He left immediately and never returned.

At the time Brinkerhoff did not take Reede's lost treasure story very seriously. He had spent many years packing supplies and ores to and from the mines in the mining districts of the San Juan country and had heard many lost treasure stories in that time. Brinkerhoff knew that such things could happen, and he knew that miners and mill men did appropriate high-grade ore or rich concentrates and cache them out until a convenient time to carry them away, but a story of a rich cache of bullion over forty years old seemed entirely too much of a hoary old legend to arouse his active interest. At a later date he would deeply regret his passive interest in Reede's story, but at the time and under the circumstances the story was recited to him, his reactions were the normal ones that every other experienced mountain man would have had: "good yarn, plausible, could have happened, doubtless did, but where in hell does it personally concern me?"

Reede had extended him no invitation to participate in the quest, nor had he offered him any of the rich reward in case of discovery. The discussion had been merely an informal conversation in which a stranger was seeking information about the mountain country from another stranger who knew that section of the mountains. To Brinkerhoff at the time, it had no further significance.

Brinkerhoff had work of his own to do. It was getting late in the fall in the high country and the outlying mines were laying in their winter supplies. This work gave him a full schedule of packing assignments for many days ahead. It was urgent that he get back to Silverton with his pack string that afternoon so he could pack a load of stuff to a mine in Ice Lake basin, west of town, the following day.

At the foot of Timber Hill Brinkerhoff turned his pack mules loose and headed them up the trail ahead of him. About a mile up the grade, a short distance above the Old Beaver Pond, the trail forked at a crossing on a little stream that emptied into the pond, the main trail crossed the creek and proceeded along the south bank parallel to the stream, while a dim one turned to the right along the north bank for a couple of hundred yards to another crossing farther up the draw. In the perverted way of mules, some of them crossed on the main trail while others turned up the dim trail to the right along the north bank. Brinkerhoff reined his horse onto the dim trail to follow the animals that had gone that way, to drive them back to the rest of the string. When he had gone a hundred yards or so he ran onto a "whole mess of dead quakie saplings that were blazed only on one side."

Most of them had fallen down, a few were still standing, and two had survived the fierce struggle for existence. They were fair sized trees but still bore the unmistakable marks of an old blaze. The axe marks were still very distinct on all the old blazes.

Brinkerhoff recalled his conversation with Reede a couple of hours earlier. To find so many trees blazed all in one spot, and in such a peculiar fashion, without design or pattern, was certainly something most extraordinary anywhere in the mountains. To satisfy this natural curiosity Brinkerhoff looked for the other markings and specific landmarks that the old man had mentioned, and he found them all—the three big rocks in the open spot surrounded by mountain willow, the spruce tree at the point of rock on the creek bank, the big tree with the big blaze by the side of the trail, and the timbered knob with ledges of rimrock.

"Too bad the old man didn't come along with me," mused the veteran packer to himself, "he would have found out where the marks are, then he could have used his knowledge of where to dig." And with that bit of philosophy Brinkerhoff turned his horse up the trail behind his string of mules, steadily plodding ahead on the long climb in order to be on time for a $50 packing job on the morrow, while not fifty yards away from him lay $60,000 in gold bullion just waiting to be picked up.

Brinkerhoff would visit that spot again in later years in company with the writer, and together they would get much closer to that elusive golden hoard.

Reede was not a talkative man, particularly about his cache of gold bullion, but he did tell two other men about it a couple of days before he talked to Brinkerhoff. Pat Duncan and Rusty Makibbon were a couple of young cowboys and range riders in the area who had set up their temporary camp on the same campgrounds on the Rio Grande at the mouth of Squaw creek just below the Farmers' Union dam, where Reede was camping. Reede got acquainted with the young fellows and visited with them around the campfire in the evenings.

On one of these occasions he related to them substantially the same story he later told to Brinkerhoff, and he just astutely avoided telling them where the gold was buried with relation to the signs. He did not mention Timber Hill by name because, as noted previously, he did not know about the name of that particular place. Duncan and Makibbon were not as familiar with the country above the Farmers' Union lake as they were with that below it. They knew there was a trail up there that crossed over to Silverton, Duncan had been over it once but that was not sufficient to familiarize him with many of its details. About all the information they could give him was that the trail was no longer a wagon road, and that it turned off from some of the other trails somewhere above the lake. Reede did not press them for more detailed information that evening, and they left the campground the next morning. Reede had been hunting for that turn-off trail, trying to determine which one of several trails it might be, when he encountered Brinkerhoff.

Reede's story about his buried treasure became an interesting topic of conversation between Duncan and Makibbon. They discussed it quite a bit both pro and con. They had no doubts about the truth of the old man's yarn; they planned to make a trip over the old trail at some future time when opportunity offered and hunt for that treasure themselves.

Duncan's interest in the buried treasure got quite a boost one evening around the campfire on the fall roundup the following year. He had recounted Reede's story to his camp companion, an old-timer in the San Juan country by the name of Hink Dolff. Dolff had worked in the Silverton district and on the head of the Rio Grande in the early Nineties. He had personal knowledge of many of the events that occurred there at that time. He showed more than a passive interest in Duncan's recounting of Reede's yarn and particularly to the part about Reede hiding the dead burro's pack saddle in a spruce tree:

"Pat, I'll bet I found that very saddle right where Reede left it," he exclaimed. "I was over on the Rio Grande in the summer of '89 or '90. I was foolin' along up the trail on Timber Hill, jest killin' time, waitin' for a couple of other fellers to overtake me, when I saw an old pack saddle hangin' down from a limb of a big spruce growin' on a steep knob right by the trail. It was about two or three hundred feet up the hill from the trail. It was sure curious to see a pack saddle hangin' in such an odd place. So I clumb up there to get it. The pack rats had chewed on the leather straps and had cut the canvass britchen' all to pieces which showed that saddle had been hangin' there a long time. And it sure fits in with Reede's story, the same as some stories I heerd around Silverton at the time.

"According to those reports, a couple of fellers made a rich haul of gold bullion from a smelter over around Ophir somwhar' and pulled out from there in the night and made a clean getaway. It seems a big snowstorm came before the bullion was missed at the smelter, and covered up all the tracks so the authorities couldn't follow those guys. The rumors said they got somewhar between $50,000 and $75,000 in that haul and that they had three burros and was seen passin' by Silverton; but that was all that ever came of the matter so far as I ever heered. They got clean away. What I heered then fits in with what you just told me. Just as sure as shootin' that old saddle I found was the one Reede left and that gold is buried around thar somewhar close by. It might pay us to go up thar next summer and have a look."

So Duncan and Dolff—they left Makibbon out—went up to Timber Hill the following July on their treasure hunt. They found the spot all right, and Dolff pointed out the exact tree in which he had found the old pack saddle; and they found the other markings and landmarks Reede had mentioned. They dug a few holes here and there but they did not find the gold. They didn't "know exactly where to dig" as Reede said he would.

"Just diggin' here, by guess and by god, hain't gettin' us no whar, Pat, so we jest as well quit and go home," concluded Dolff. So home they went, and left behind them a fortune in gold bullion buried under a few inches of leafmold on an exact spot where both of them had stood at one time in their quest for it.

The writer had spent many years as a rangeman, packer, and miner in the San Juan country. I knew almost every stockman, packer, and range rider in the country, and a good many of the old timers like Hink Dolff. I was well acquainted with Pat Duncan; and Brinkerhoff and I had been friends and associates since early boyhood. Duncan related to me the story of the cache of bullion on Timber Hill when we were both working on the same livestock outfit, over in the Pagosa district; and later I added other bits of information as my work carried me from one section of the country to another. It all fit into a very definite pattern. I did not hunt for the cache during that time, however. I did ride several miles out of my way on one trip to Silverton in order to travel up the trail on Timber Hill just to see if I could recognize the spot. I had no trouble picking it out.

Several years later Brinkerhoff and I were working a lease on The Good Hope Mine at the head of Bear creek above historic old Beartown, about seven or eight miles west of Timber Hill. Brinkerhoff and I had previously discussed Reede's story and the other information we had gathered about the cache. To satisfy our curiosity we took a week end off from our work at the mine one September and went treasure hunting for four bars of gold bullion down on Timber Hill. That gold had increased 75% in values since Reede cached it there. At that time it was worth only $20 an ounce, but when we were hunting for it its value had been increased by presidential decree to $35 per ounce; so instead of a little over $50,000 we were hunting for almost $90,000—a prize well worth trying for.

We were optimists. We took our whole pack string, consisting of nine big jacks, and our camp outfit with us. We didn't figure on finding enough gold to load all of our burros, but we did figure on knowing where all of our jacks were while we were away from the Good Hope, and not having to spend a week hunting up the ones we might have left behind.

As I look back now I think that was the only sound bit of logic we used on that entire expedition. All of us are familiar with the old adage, "If our foresight was as good as our hindsight, we would all be rich"; but on some occasions a man is so stupid, and so mentally blind to the obvious in a given set of circumstances, that I think he should be thankful even to be credited with brains enough to have "hindsight." When he looks back on what occurred, and reflects how different it could have been if——, he feels like he hasn't enough intellect to be a first rate moron. That is what happened to us.

We had no trouble finding the place. We were as familiar with Timber Hill and all other sections of the mountains in that area as most folk are with their back yard. Just as a matter of course, we rechecked all signs and markings—the timbered knob with its series of rock ledges, the big tree on it where Dolff had found the old pack saddle, the tree with the big blaze by the trail, the blazed aspens (both those that were fallen and partially decayed and the few that were still standing), and the spruce with the ends of its branches cut off. Everything tallied.

"Now, we got the marks. If we were as smart as Reede, we'd know exactly where to dig to get the gold," remarked Brinkerhoff, "but since we ain't that smart we'll just have to dig where we figure the bullion might be."

Other gold seekers ahead of us had already done that very thing at several different places around there. Someone had burrowed all around in the shallow, rocky soil among the roots of the spruce tree with the cut branches; others had dug trenches around the base of the three big rocks in the marshy, open spot opposite Reede's old campsite. These trenches had since filled with seep water which made those big boulders look like medieval castles surrounded by moats. Other little pot holes had been dug at different places around there—some of them in the most absurd and crazy spots imaginable, but men will do crazy things when hunting for gold. One fellow had even used a charge of dynamite to break deeper into the solid rock in the bottom of a shallow hole he had dug for the treasure, evidently working on the theory that the gold was underneath it although Reede had nothing but a light shovel with which to dig a pit for his bullion, and a very limited time to do it in. But, as I said before, men will do crazy things when looking for gold, and some of those crazy acts are for things he doesn't do which he should. You will see what I mean presently.

Apparently all the hunting for Reede's buried treasure had been done in the area across the little creek from his camp, and in the immediate vicinity of his old markings. This all seemed logical because this strip was easily accessible to his camp, and was a convenient spot to hide his gold in. He was in a hurry the morning he cached it, and he was in a snow storm; it seemed logical that he would choose the easiest place to get to. This spot was it. Therefore the bullion must be somewhere in it. Wonderful logic? All we had to do was find that "somewhere."

We set about our task in a systematic manner. We blocked the area off into sections and explored each section thoroughly before going on to the next one. We did not dig holes in our searching, although we had tools to dig with. We did it by probing with a light steel rod which we had sharpened for that purpose. We could work a lot faster that way; and we knew from experience, just as any other man who has worked with tools in the mines or in the soil, that we could tell by the "feel" of our probe whether we were driving it into ground that had been previously disturbed or not; and when the probe hit an obstacle we could detect with a high degree of certainty the nature of that obstacle, whether it was a root, a piece of metal, loose stone, or solid rock; and in case of any doubt we could always excavate and make certain what it was.

We probed along for an hour or so and were beginning to get bored with the procedure. Even probing for gold can become tiresome and mundane when one follows the same routine long enough, without a break of some kind in the monotony. We were about ready to quit for a time when Brinkerhoff's probe hit a chunk of metal of some kind about a foot under the ground and right by the side of the dim, old trail on the north side of the creek—the same one his mules had followed years before when he found the blazed aspens. The spot looked like a very favorable one for a cache. There was a tone of excitement in his voice as he hollered to me:

"I've hit a chunk of metal of some kind, and it ain't iron." I have hunted for gold a whole lot in my life, and I have found some of it during that time and have had many thrills in my exciting quests, but the thrill I experienced on this occasion was the greatest and the most exciting I ever had! It was wonderful!

I was probing a spot several feet away but in a few jumps I was by Brinkerhoff's side.

"Levi, this might be it. Let me try it," as I grabbed his probe for a tap or two with my own hammer to test the discovery for myself.

"It sure is metal," I exclaimed as visions of $90,000 worth of gold bullion filled my mind. "Let's dig it out and see what it is." With that excited ejaculation I dropped on my knees and started to scratch up the ground with my hands. A man will sure do crazy things when he is hunting for gold!

I didn't realize how foolish I was acting until Brinkeroff brought me to my senses with the remark: "Hey, what the hell did we bring a shovel for, if not to dig with?"

"It's over at camp. I'll go and get it. Hold this spot 'til I get back," just as though that spot, with a steel probe in it, would get lost in the few minutes it would take to get back with the shovel—a man will even say crazy things when he is hunting for gold.

At camp our axe was leaning against a tree, out in plain sight, but the shovel was lying on the ground behind the tree. I grabbed the axe and started back.

"We dig with a shovel, not an axe," Brinkerhoff hollered at me.

"I guess I am kinda excited," I explained as I exchanged the axe for the shovel.

"Not just kinda," humorously replied Levi. "You are as excited as hell. Might just as well keep your shirt on for a while yet. This stuff may not be gold."

And that stuff was not gold. It was a chunk of babbitt metal —the material that was formerly used quite extensively to line machine bearings. It had perhaps been lost off from a pack at that spot many years before and had gradually gotten buried in the ground there. This was one occasion when lead, not in the lethal form of bullets, injected excitements into a hunt for buried gold.

It was past midafternoon that Brinkerhoff and I sat on the mountainside opposite the timbered knob back of Reede's old campsite. We had done all the probing and hunting for the buried bullion on the north side of the creek that we had time for. We had to get back to the Good Hope Mine that evening.

"How would that hillside over there be for the cache," asked Brinkerhoff as his gaze took in the steep, rough slope with its broken, rock ledges and narrow benches.

"It don't appeal to me as being a likely place," I replied. "It is steep as hell, and there is not much dirt on those benches to bury anything in. Besides Reede was in a hurry the morning he hid that gold, and it was snowing, too. It don't make sense that he would carry that bullion up there under those circumstances."

"Guess you are right," said he, "but let's go up there and give it a quick 'once over'."

We did. The hillside looked so uninviting to us for the possible location of a cache that we did not even carry our probing tools up there with us. We climbed up through the broken spot in the ledges and casually looked over each narrow bench which had an accumulation of leafmold and soil on it. We saw nothing to arouse our curiosity or that we thought merited our investigation. About two thirds of the way up to the top, we again came to the tree where Dolff had found the old pack saddle. We stood on the narrow bench at the base of that tree and looked over the area below where Reede had made his markings on the trees, and where we had spent the day in fruitless search for the bullion he had so effectively hidden. In fact we sat down there and smoked a cigarette.

Each of us was trying to put himself in Reede's stead, and trying to figure what we would do under the circumstances. It was some of that old familiar stuff about "now if I was in your place I would do it this way, etc.," but we were not in Reede's stead and we did not have his personality. What we would do under those circumstances was one thing and what Reede did was quite another.

"I wish now I'd asked Reede more about that cache when he told me about it," remarked Brinkerhoff. "He might not 'uve told me any more than he did, but maybe I could have found something that would be of help now. But I never dreamed then that I would ever be hunting for his bullion."

"Well, we are not doing any good sitting here, so let's get on back up to the mine." We did not know that we were, right then, sitting on the hottest seat we would ever have. Just some more of that crazy stuff in the crazy game of hunting gold.

We went back up to the Good Hope Mine and to work there until the snow ran us out of the mountains that fall. We didn't find any gold there either. Brinkerhoff went to a railroad job in California, and I went to work as a reporter for the late John Young on the old Durango *News*.

The following summer I was alone on the Good Hope except for a few short periods when I could hire some man to help me. No one cared to stay out in that isolated place very long at a time. The war was coming and employment was easy to get, and I found it difficult to find a steady hand that was looking for work—not just employment at big wages. I was alone up there a good part of the time.

I spoke Spanish and got well acquainted with the Mexican

sheepherders and camp tenders who were looking after flocks of sheep that pastured in the vicinity. I had a radio that had good reception, which was something exceptional among those mineralized, rocky peaks on the north flank of the Needle Mountains; and, more important, I had a good "hair cutting" outfit (tonsorial tools). The Mexican herders and camp tenders took turns, especially on Sundays, visiting me at the mine in order to hear the radio, to get a hair cut, or to repair their equipment in my blacksmith shop; and they brought me many a piece of fresh mutton in exchange for these small favors. All of that good fellowship made life pretty pleasant that summer. The Mexicans were greatly interested in my mining activities, and in gold, and inevitably their conversations turned to lost mines and buried treasures. One of the camp tenders, Crescencio Martinez, who lived down near La Jara in the lower San Luis Valley, became particularly interested in my story about the lost gold bullion on Timber Hill. He seemed to be a sort of "bell weather" among the sheepherders in the Beartown district and made weekly trips down Timber Hill to Cochran's Dude Ranch at the upper end of the Farmers' Union Lake where sheep owners had a sort of supply storage, and where letters could be sent to the post office and accumulated mail for the herders could be picked up.

The Good Hope was located high up on the Continental Divide, away above timber line. All of our mining timbers and our firewood had to be packed up from the timber down around old Beartown. We needed some timbers, so one morning late in August I set out to round up my burros to pack up some timbers. Normally I would have found them down in the old Beartown meadow about a mile and a half from the mine; but not so this morning. Someone had left the gate open in the drift fence at the lower end of the meadow, and my burros had gone through it and down Bear creek to the Rio Grande. I expected to find them on the grassy flat between Bear creek and the Rio Grande where the two streams came together; but I got fooled. Instead of stopping there, my jacks had crossed the main stream and had taken out down the old trail over Timber Hill. Some other careless person had left the gate open in the second drift fence on the lower boundary of the cattle range at the top of Timber Hill, so

I did not find my jacks there. I had already followed the rascals five or six miles, so I was pretty much out of sorts as I started the long hike down the hill after them. And I was really in foul humor when I got to the foot of the hill and saw my jacks standing contentedly in the shade of some willows about 200 yards down the meadow. It was easily twelve miles back to the mine.

There was a passable automobile road that came from the main highway at the Farmers' Union Reservoir around over some ridges and up to a nice camping place at the head of the valley right at the foot of the trail. A couple of young men, about thirty years old, had just driven into this camping place and were setting up their camp there, not more than forty yards from the trail when I came barging out of the timber. They were driving a light car with a Nebraska license. I saw them and they saw me, but I was too mad to be civil to anyone just them. I waved a salute to them and went on after those provoking jackasses. I regretted afterwards, and very shortly afterwards, that I did not cultivate acquaintances with those guys. Right then I did not want to cultivate anything but the tail ends of those burros with a hard twisted rope.

I caught old Jug Head, the biggest, toughest, and fastest jack in the lot, and got astraddle of him and took in after the rest of those exasperating rascals and we started up the trail for home. As I left the road and started up the trail in the timber at the foot of the hill, I heard one of those young fellows remark to the other one: "Evidently that is the trail we are looking for right there where that man went with those jackasses."

"It may be. We will have a look up there after dinner." At the time I attached no significance either to the men or to their remarks. Campers and fishermen were common in this section during the summer months, and to me these two were no different from many others I had seen there. I went on to the mine.

About dusk the next evening my friend Crescencio came riding up to my cabin. Before he said a word I could sense that he was tense and surcharged with excitement.

"Por vida suyo companero," he fairly sputtered. "Yo tengo nuevadades de muy grande importancia." ("For the life of you! pardner, I have news of greatest importance.")

"Si, que pasa?" ("Yes, what is it?")

Crescencio was so wrought up that I began to get excited myself although I did not know what on earth about.

"Han hallegdo el entierro alla en la questa." ("They have found the cache of gold down there on the Hill.")

Then I did get excited, but this time I knew what about.

"Cuando lo hallaron?" ("When did they find it?")

"Hoy" ("Today.")

"Quien lo hallo?" ("Who found it?")

"Dos hombres con campo en la pie de la questa." ("Two men camped at the foot of the grade.")

"Two men camped at the foot of the hill," that sentence hit me like a diesel locomotive. They were the guys I had seen the day before setting up their camp where I had found my burros.

Here is what happened, as Crescencio narrated it to me in Spanish, and I translate it into proper English:

"I went down to the store this morning to mail some letters, get our mail and some cigarettes. Down below the Beaver Pond, almost at the foot of the hill, I met a couple of young Americans coming up the trail. One of them was carrying a rifle and the other one had a shovel. One of them had a little pack in a sack on his back. I saw them quite a way down the trail before they saw me. They kept looking at the marks on all the trees along the trail, and at the hillsides on both sides all along. I knew from the way they acted that they were not hunters or fishermen, but that they were hunting for something else along the trail. Then I remembered about the 'entierro' (cache) and suspicioned they might be looking for that.

"When they saw me they quit looking and pointing around, and just waited for me to go on by. They said 'Good Morning' but did not say anything more, and I didn't try to talk to them. I went on down the trail and I saw their camp right at the foot of the hill. I did not tell anyone at the store about seeing these two men. I did not talk to anyone very much down there because no one there speaks Mexican, and I din't understand much English. I left the store a little after noon to return to my camp.

"I looked very closely to see if those men had returned to their camp when I came by it but they were not there. I looked for their tracks in the trail when I started up it, but I could only see footprints going up the trail—none coming back down it. I kept a good 'lookout' for them all the way up past the Beaver Pond to where the trail crosses that little creek just below the timbered knob where the 'entierro' was supposed to be. There I heard men talking. It sounded like they were over on the side of the timbered knob. They were talking in English so I could not understand anything they were saying. I did not cross the creek on the main trail there but took that dim, old trail among the willows on the north bank. I got up almost to the edge of that little open spot where the blazed aspen trees are. From there I could see those two men digging in the leafmold on a little bench at the base of a tree almost at the top of the knob. They had not yet seen me.

"When I saw them lift some bricks of yellow metal out of the hole they had dug, I knew they had found that 'entierro' and it made my heart sad that it was not you who found it.

"Then my horse, he moved one little bit to chase a fly off his nose, and those Americanos saw me. One of them jumped up quick and grabbed his rifle and pointed it at me and shouted something real sharp in English. I was afraid he was going to shoot me, so I spurred my horse very quick and he jumped forward into a run and I got away. So now I came here to tell you what I saw. What can we do about it?"

I was so dumfounded, so surprised, by Crescencio's story that I had temporarily lost my wits. The story seemed ludicrous, incredible, yet I knew the Mexican was telling me the truth as he had seen it, and I knew that two young Americans were camped down at the foot of the hill.

"Cris, there isn't anything we can do about it tonight. We can go down there in the morning and look things over, but beyond that there is nothing we can do. If they have found the gold it is theirs and that is that."

I didn't sleep very well that night. If the story Crescencio had told me was true, Brinkerhoff and I had missed a $90,000 fortune by the thinnest margin. I was anxious for morning to come so I could go down and see for myself.

Cris came over to my cabin early the next morning and we got on our way to Timber Hill.

Cris's story was true. We found the pit, a trench about four feet long, from which four objects of some kind had been removed. There were four separate and distinct imprints where those square objects had lain for so many years, and the hole was just fresh dug. I know it was not there "the day before yesterday" when I passed by there with my burros. Cris and I slipped on down to the foot of the trail to see if the men and their camp were still there, but they were not and the firepit was stone cold. Those boys had pulled out the night before, and by this time they were many miles away.

The pit from which they had taken that bullion was on the narrow bench at the base of the "old packsaddle tree" where Brinkerhoff and I had tramped around, and had then sat down to smoke a cigarette, while we speculated on the spot where that cache might be. We were sitting on top of the blamed thing right then!

Imprints of the bars of bullion in the trench showed that the gold was covered with not more than three inches of leafmold, but even that thin covering was sufficient to conceal it from me and Brinkerhoff. That hillside did not look like an inviting place for a cache to me, so I did not really hunt for it there. I merely gave it "the once over." The fact that it did not have an appealing appearance as a caching place should have made it obvious that that would be the best place to hunt for the cache of bullion. When a man hides something, he does so to keep some other man from finding it; and obviously he is going to hide it where he believes the other fellow will not look. That is what Reede did with that gold bullion, but I was too stupid to see the obvious.

Had Brinkerhoff and I taken our probing rods along with us up that hillside, we would have probed into the shallow leafmold on those ledges just as a matter of habit, and as sure as the due date on an installment payment, we would have struck those bars of hidden gold. I still am convinced that men do crazy things when hunting for gold.

Who the men were that got the cache of gold bullion, where they came from, and where they went, I never found out, neither did anyone else in the San Juan country, so far as I know. The only clues I ever obtained to their identity was that their car was a light Chevrolet with Nebraska license plates, and that one of the men remarked to a fisherman he encountered along the highway by the Farmers' Union Reservoir, that his grandfather had crossed over the divide from Silverton to the Rio Grande with some pack burros in the early days, and that one of those burros had died somewhere along that route, making it necessary for his grandfather to throw some of his stuff away.

Whoever they were, they knew what they were looking for, and they knew "exactly where to dig" when they found that spot. Reede was the only living man that possessed that knowledge, and he must have, before he died, given that information to at least one of the fellows who found that gold; because it sure did not take them long, nor require much of their time and effort, to do the job. They made $90,000 easy.

My $40,000 Dinner

I have never been much given to expensive meals, or to expensive foods. My greatest problem has always been to get enough even of the common kind. I have done fairly well, however, because in more than forty years spent on the range I have never yet really missed a meal, although I have postponed many a one. I still have quite a backlog of meals to be made up for whenever I get the opportunity, and the grub to do it with.

It isn't the meals I have missed, however, that linger in my memory nearly so much as some that I didn't miss. One of these was a simple camp dinner of "hellfired stew," which I cooked myself for myself over a small campfire one day in August, 1937, by a little creek deep in the Rockies on the headwaters of the Rio Grande in southwestern Colorado. (A hellfired stew is a favorite diet with range men because it is easy to prepare and "stays with the ribs.") It consists of small pieces of fresh mutton, potatoes, and onions all fried together in the same pan, and eaten while hot. Some variations can be made in the preparation of the food. Chili is sometimes added—whether as an aid to the flavor or to the hellfire is problematical.

It was not the ingredients in my dinner that made it so valuable or so outstanding. In actual cash I don't suppose it cost more than forty cents, and I suspect on that particular day a lot of other sheepherders and rangemen were eating the same kind of dinner that I was. But they were not eating under the same circumstances I was, or, at least, not off the same kind of table—and that is an important difference.

At that time I was the *caporal*, or range foreman for the Hersch Investment Company of Pagosa Springs. In other words, I was the general roustabout on the company's livestock outfits, which, that particular summer, consisted of several herds of sheep ranging on scattered allotments for a hundred miles along the Continental Divide between the San Juan and the Rio Grande watersheds. This was all high country and on the National Forest. It was a "primitive area," and was all pack country, where the only means of transportation was on horseback or by pack animal. In order to get about over the country to attend to my work, I had my own saddle horse, pack mule, and individual little camp outfit. I stayed in the regular camp when it was convenient, but camped out alone when necessary. At best it was several miles from any of our camps down to the highway either on Williams creek on the San Juan side, or to the Farmers' Union Reservoir on the Rio Grande side, where stock salt and supplies for the camps could be delivered by truck, there to be picked up by our camp tenders with their burros. It was a part of my job to arrange for the rendezvous between the campmen and the supply truck. This was also a strip of mountain country rich in treasure trove. Stories were numerous of old Spanish mines, rich ones, lost or hidden, lo, these many years, and of buried treasures and small caches of rich gold ore and of bullion. According to legend there was a fabulously rich, old Spanish mine somewhere on the head of Ute creek, a tributary of the Rio Grande, and just across the Continental Divide from the headwaters of the Pine, the Flint Fork, and the Vallacito on the San Juan side. "Two sleeps" down the Divide east from this mine was said to be a major cache of rich ore made by the old Spanish more than a century before.

And in the environs of the mine were said to be several small caches of extra rich gold ore which the old Spaniards had purposely selected and hidden away from the mine as a precaution against a raid by the Indians—to be transported out to Taos by the Spaniards themselves on their last trip out of the mountains in the autumn.

Tangible evidence in support of these legends and treasure stories was an abundance of old Spanish markings and signs in the area. Measurement of the new growth on the old tree blazes established their age circa 170 years, and subsequent tests of some of them by tree-ring chronology corroborated this estimate. This would set the date when those markings were made at about 1770, more or less. And those markings conformed to a definite pattern and a definite system. Sometimes their arrangement seemed mysterious—always interesting, always intriguing. I was constantly on the watch out for some spot I thought likely for one of those caches of gold.

Interest of all of us local stockmen in the treasure trove of our bailiwick received added stimulation almost every summer season by the advent of anywhere from one to four or five different treasure-hunting parties in our area. Some of these parties were small, consisting of two or three men; others would have five to seven individuals in the group. Some of these parties, usually the smaller ones, went about their business seriously, others were out for a lark and had a lot of fun while they did some hunting for treasure. All of them screened their mission under the guise of "fishing." It was mighty easy for us to distinguish between the two classes.

It is pretty difficult for anyone to fool the combined observation and watchfulness of all the sheepherders in any district. A sheepherder is highly skilled in observing the action and the tracks of all animals, including man, in his territory, and interpreting what he sees. Being a sheepherder myself, I knew all the other herders and campmen in the whole area, whether they were working for the Hersch Investment Company or not. Exchange of knowledge among ourselves about the "going-ons" in our district made interesting campfire conversation. And sheepherders like to talk—most of them do.

The general area that attracted some of the more serious treasure hunters was Ute creek and that section of the Continental Divide along the head of the Vallacito, Flint Fork, and Pine. This district lay on the upper end of my territory. I made several trips through it every summer. The Divide runs almost due east and west through this strip of country.

Ute creek lies on the north, or Rio Grande, side of the divide, and the Pine, Flint Fork, and other tributaries of the San Juan are on the south side. The trail from the Pine follows up El Rincon La Osa, a beautiful alpine basin, crosses the ridge to Flint Fork, and then turns north across the Continental Divide and down past Ute Lake, a famous "fishing hole," right at timberline on a little tributary of Middle Ute creek. From Ute Lake the trail winds down about a half mile through a band of fine spruce timber to the head of a long, open little mountain valley. About fifty yards west from the point where the trail came out into this park was an excellent camping place at the base of a big, dead spruce tree. That tree was a big one. It must have been three and a half to four feet in diameter and over 100 feet tall. That tree had been there a long time. It stood on a bit of high ground right by the riverlet, and there was not an artificial mark on it; at its north base was a big, almost flat rock that resembled the upper half of a giant hot-dog bun, laid out there, partially buried in the ground, to serve as a natural dining table. How such an odd-looking rock, one so unusual in that locality, ever got in such an unusual position I never stopped to figure. There was not another rock like it anywhere near about.

On this particular August day I was on my way through the Ute creek area to meet the supply truck at the upper end of the Farmers' Union Reservoir on the Rio Grande. I had instructed one of our campmen on El Rincon La Osa to bring his pack burros and meet me the following morning at the reservoir to pick up his supplies. He would follow the same trail I traveled.

Following my usual custom, I camped for my noon meal at the base of this big spruce tree in the head of that little valley. I cooked my hellfired stew on a small campfire near that flat rock, and used the stone for a table to eat my dinner on. I thought nothing of the incident. I had done the same thing many times before.

That summer there was a party of three men hunting treasure on the Ute creek area. These fellows were in the "serious" classification. They were really different from any other group we had seen in the district that year. All the sheepherders were interested in their movements and kept a pretty close collective tab on them. These same men had spent a part of the previous summer exploring around in the same area. Their return engagement in 1937 was, to say the least, very intriguing and aroused intense curiosity. They had been in the district since mid-July.

Ostensibly they were fishermen. They always set their camp in the edge of the timber along the open valleys of West Ute creek or of the Middle Ute, and they always carried their fishing gear very plainly in sight whenever they left their camp, but no one ever saw them cast a line into any of the streams; instead they

Turkey Head Mt. (Silverton).

Typical early day gold melt house to recover mercury from gold
amalgam (Liberty Bell Mill, Telluride).

Silverton, Colorado. Carson sold his gold here to a smelter.

An early day smelter, near Silverton. *State Historical Society of Colorado.*

Big Turkey Mountain. Carson's body found near
here alongside his pack mules.

139

General area of Carson Mine. West Needles Mountains.

Rocky formation near Carson Mine.

Molas Lake (Silverton), near lost mines of that area.

View of Engineer Mountain from Coal Bank Hill. Near Molas
Lake, Baker Brothers' seam.

Silverton, Colorado, winter scene.

Summer scene, near Baker Brothers' seam.

Needle Mountains, early spring, Carson mine near. Shadow is burro's ear.

Ophir Pass. Golden Fortune of Timber Hill went over this pass on mule back.

Work of treasure hunters under spruce tree, Golden Fortune of Timber Hill.

Piedra River headwaters, on Four Mile Creek.

Upper Piedra River. Route of Stewart.

would hide their tackle behind a tree or in a convenient clump of brush in the edge of the timber some distance away from their camp and would then begin to hunt for signs and markings on trees or rocks all along the little gullies on the mountainsides. They would retrieve their tackle on their return trip to their camp, so they were always carrying fishing gear when they were out in the open and likely to be seen. In their searching they would go as high as timberline but never scouted above that point. Whatever they were hunting was evidently in the timber.

These fellows were not men of mystery. They were human, even as you and I. They were Americans, men of middle age and not uncivil in their conduct. They passed the time of day pleasantly with any of us fellows they met; they were merely unsociable and skilfully avoided meeting other fellows most of the time. They tended to their own business and didn't intend to let anyone else attend to it for them. They enforced that provision with a Winchester on one of my campmen one morning.

I saw these men along the trail in the edge of the timber pretty well down on Middle Ute creek about mid-afternoon after I had eaten my dinner at the base of the dead spruce tree. They passed the time of day pleasantly enough with me but gave no indication that they wanted any further conversation. They went their way and I went mine.

Early the next morning my campman, Pedro Abeyta, from our camp on Rincon La Osa, came down the same trail with his burros from Ute Lake that I had followed the day before, but he encountered a different greeting at the head of the little, open valley than I had. As he emerged with his burros from the timber into the opening, he was greeted by a man with a Winchester who wasted no time on the little civilities of life, but gruffly told Abeyta to "stay on the trail and keep riding."

To say that Abeyta was startled by such a sudden and unusual encounter in those peaceful mountains would be a gross understatement. He was downright scared. Needless to say he kept riding but he also had a good look while he was going by.

What he saw made news—at least it made news in sheepherder circles. Over at the base of the big, dead spruce tree the men had lifted up that flat rock and had turned it completely over and

The Stewart Placer

All dirt is not cheap. The dirt found by Captain R. E. Stewart in the San Juan mountains of southwestern Colorado was not. It was valuable—worth $80,000 per ton at that time and there were unlimited tons of it. It would be almost twice as valuable today, and all of it would meet with ready sale.

The Stewart Placer is one of the most famous lost treasures of the San Juan country. It is the "Adams Diggins" of southwestern Colorado—a fabulously rich treasure of coarse placer gold and big nuggets that would rival in extent the treasure of the famous placer that Adams found—and lost. The existence of the Stewart Placer is well authenticated and the section of the country in which it was found is a well established fact. But more of this as the story progresses.

Stewart was a captain in the United States Cavalry in the early days of the West and was every inch a military man of the old school. He was tall, slender of build, quick in his movements, mentally alert, and decisive in his decisions. He was a superb horseman and a capable cavalry officer. He had a good education and had worked his way up through the ranks to a captaincy.

Early in June, 1852, Captain Stewart, with a small detachment of cavalrymen, fully equipped with camp outfit and pack mules, arrived at the little Mexican settlement of Abiquiu, New Mexico, an outpost of civilization on the Rio Grande river. Stewart, with his party, was on a military mission to northern California. Rather than take the southern route across the hot, dry, desert sections of Arizona and California, Stewart chose to follow the Old Spanish Trail through the mountains of southwestern Colorado and across Utah to Sacramento. This travelway had been used by the early Spaniards in exploring and mining gold in this region for over a century and a half; and in the early 1800's William Wolfskill and other enterprising traders of Santa Fe organized regular parties that used this travelway extensively for two decades in the California trade. For a time it was an important artery of western commerce. Big pack trains of mules in charge of a well organized company of experienced men, loaded with blankets, bolts of cloth, shoes, sugar, and other staple commodities of trade, made frequent trips from Santa Fe over the Old Spanish Trail to California where the goods were sold or exchanged for Spanish mules, raw furs, silks from the orient, and for gold, both dust and bullion. Vast treasure was transported over the old trail for a time in its heyday but not all of this treasure arrived at its proper destination. The Indians prevented that.

The Utes, a powerful tribe of mountain Indians, roamed over southwestern Colorado and far out into Utah at that time and claimed all of this vast and fertile domain as their home. When aroused they were a savage lot, skilled in mountain warfare, and were as cunning an adversary as the whites had ever encountered. In the late 1820's the Utes went on the warpath and began to raid the packtrains on this route. They massacred the men in charge and appropriated the merchandise and the animals for themselves. A few signs of these old encounters are still to be seen in some of the forested areas in the mountains of southwestern Colorado. Old bones of animals and of men, arrow points embedded in old spruce trees, bullet marks and an occasional rusted bit of metal—an old spur or a part of an old firearm or a skinning knife characteristic of the period—has been found at these spots as mute witnesses of the battles that occurred there. The writer has found three such places. The opposition of the savage Utes put an effective end to the use of the Old Spanish Trail by white men for several years. By 1852, however, the Utes had become a little less aggressive, and Captain Stewart determined to follow this route to California. It was still dangerous territory, but Stewart figured that by being careful not to encounter any Indian bands and by traveling fast he and his party could make it through.

He camped at Abiquiu a couple of days to gather additional information from the old settlers there about the route he was to follow. Some of the information he had previously obtained about the old trail was conflicting and just didn't seem to fit. He wanted to get his directions and other essential data cleared up before he

148

started on his way through that vast, uncharted, and unsettled region. His earlier informants had confused the Old Spanish trail with the route followed by Father Escalante on his famous expedition through southwestern Colorado in 1776 in an unsuccessful attempt to find a way from Santa Fe to the Catholic Missions in California. The two trails are not the same. At Abiquiu, Stewart got his information properly straightened out. He got his trail untangled from that of Escalante and was ready to proceed on his way.

During the afternoon of the second day he was in Abiquiu, a Mexican youth, Mariano Garcia, about 16 years old and an orphan, approached the Captain at his camp.

"Senior Capitan, I lika join your companea and go it wisa you to de California," said the youth in his broken English.

Stewart was surprised at this offer. He could not accept volunteers even if he had wanted to, and he didn't want to accept this lad, this strip of a boy, for such a hard and dangerous trip.

"I do not want any volunteers," replied the captain, "and if I did I could not accept you without your father's consent."

"I don't got no father," the boy said. "I be un huerfano (an orphan). I leeve wis an old man who be too mean to me. I likka go wis you so I can getta far away, and no getta whipped too much. Please it to you letta me go. I helpet to do de work at the campo. Mebbe so, some time you needa me to talk de Mexicano for you."

This last point was a powerful argument for the lad, and finally Stewart consented for the youth to accompany the group but not to become a member of it. Garcia was to furnish his own horse, bedding, clothes, and gun. Stewart was to furnish the food, and young Garcia was to assist in the camp chores. And so the Mexican youth became a sort of outcast member of the party, but was to play an important part in the Stewart Placer story.

In later years Garcia returned to the San Juan country to hunt for the placer which he had helped to discover. And because he always wore typical cowboy garb—big, broadbrimmed hat, knotted scarf around his neck, high-heeled boots, spurs, and chaps— he became known as El Vaquero.

The course of the Old Spanish trail lay northwest from Abiquiu, up the Little Chama river over the Continental Divide at the head of that stream and across the San Juan river and its tributaries to ascend the big divide again at the head of Middle Fork of the Piedra river about 50 miles northwest of Pagosa Hot Springs. Along this route are two unmistakable landmarks which have no similar counterparts in all of the Southwest. They are the Pagosa Hot Springs and La Ventana. The first one is the mammoth natural hot springs on the east bank of the San Juan river where the modern little town of Pagosa now stands; the other is a very sharp and distinct natural doorway, some 200 feet high, cut in the perpendicular rock crest of the Continental Divide at the head of Pine river about seventy-five miles northwest of Pagosa Springs. La Ventana is a prominent landmark visible for many miles along the old trail, and was used by the early travelers along this route as an unmistakable guide in their course across the country.

Stewart knew about both of these landmarks. He could see La Ventana away in the distance to the northwest from the crest of the Continental Divide where he crossed it at the head of the Little Chama. He charted his course accordingly. From the information he had, he knew the approximate location of the hot springs. He had heard so much about these springs that he was particularly anxious to see them, and to bathe in their mineral waters. He found the hot springs but had no opportunity to bathe in them or to tarry long in their vicinity. He saw them, however—saw the boiling caldron where the steaming water gurgles out of the ground, and the column of vapor that perpetually rises from the springs. And he smelled them too. He got that never-to-be-forgotten odor that is an inseparable part of Pagosa Springs.

A big encampment of Indians a short distance west of the springs prevented Stewart from camping there and bathing in the natural hot water as he had intended to do. Thirty years later Stewart got his bath in Pagosa Springs.

By making a wide detour to the north, Stewart and his party avoided detection by the Utes and found a safe place to camp several miles farther on in the pine timber.

The captain and his men were on their way early the next morning. To quote El Vaquero, "We traveled steadily all day holding a north-westerly direction through a beautiful country with lots of parks, much tall, green grass, and big pine trees." That night they camped "in a well hidden place near the foot of the high mountains." They hoped to find some place on the following morning where they could climb to the summit of the divide. By following signs of an old Indian trail up a point of ridge and around a steep, heavily timbered mountainside, they succeeded in finding a gap in the rimrock and in ascending to a notch or pass in the crest of the range quite a distance above timberline.

They crossed the divide at this point and descended a long, open mountainside that was well covered with verdant, alpine vegetation, which grows so abundantly over the high mountains in this region, into a beautiful little mountain valley. Apparently this valley was no different from innumerable other similar nooks and coves along the divide. A placid little mountain brook of clear water mandered through the meadow that made the floor of the valley. Here and there along the way, other little streams having their source in springs at the base of the mountain sides flowed across the grassy bottom to join the main brook. The lower end of the valley was rather closed in by low, timbered ridges. Under a big spruce on one of these slopes, right at the edge of timberline, the party camped for dinner. A short distance below their camp was a small waterfall where the placid little brook cascaded over the protruding basaltic ledge that underlies the divide through all of this area.

Since their dinner was to be a hasty affair, just a sort of "pick-me-up" lunch to tide them over until evening, they only unloaded one pack mule—the one carrying the "kitchen." This was a trivial circumstance but perhaps saved their lives at the time. They did not know that keen, Indian eyes were at that moment carefully watching their every move. El Vacquero, being the chore boy, was sent to a little stream nearby to bring water for the noonday meal. The little creek, like several others in the valley, had its source in a big spring at the base of the mountain, and was a tributary to the main stream. It was about fifty yards from the camp.

When El Vacquero came back with the bucket of water for the camp, he also brought a handful of sand from the bottom of the shallow creek to show to Captain Stewart.

At the time Stewart was attending to his horse several feet away from the camp. The young Mexican addressed him with the remark: "Senior Captain, looka, the sand from the retito (creek). He be different from other sand I ever see. He is black and he es jellow. Mebbe so, he es gold."

One quick glance at the moist bit of sand in the Mexican's extended hand was sufficient to convince Stewart that it was gold!—free gold generously interspersed with black sand which might also be rich in gold.

The discovery was an unexpected surprise and a big shock to Captain Stewart, but he suppressed any outward signs of his emotions.

"Could be gold," he remarked to the Mexican with a coolness that he did not feel. "I'll take a sample along and have it assayed in Sacramento, and then we will know for sure what it is. Don't mention this to any of the other men."

The last statement was a command which, from the tone of the captain's voice, the youth knew he better obey. And he did.

The possibility of discovering gold on this trip through the mountains had never entered into Stewart's mind. He was on a military mission, not a prospecting trip, and the accomplishing of his mission was the all-important thing to him. He was on military duty so was not free to hunt gold or to exploit any discovery he might make.

He realized the precariousness of the situation, and the consequences that might follow if the soldiers with him found out about the Mexican's discovery. Hence his order for silence.

He did, however, get a small buckskin pouch out of his saddle pocket and go down to the creek to investigate for himself.

The sample the Mexican had, rich though it was, had not sufficiently prepared him for the magnitude of the discovery. To his amazement, he saw the whole creek bottom covered with grains of gold. Particles of it were thickly interspersed in the sand. Many of them were larger than grains of wheat, others were as big as kernels of corn; and there was so much fine gold mixed in the black sand that it gave a yellow cast to the whole mass. Captain Stewart was looking on a fortune of untold millions deposited there in nature's own treasure house, but under the circumstances, he could do nothing about it.

He and his party were few in number, traveling through hostile territory on a long journey. Their lives and the success of their mission depended upon their ability to travel fast through rough terrain. If they stopped, even for a short time, in any one spot they were sure to be discovered and killed by the Indians. Their pack animals were already loaded as heavy as was practical with indispensable camp equipment and food supplies. In order to pack any appreciable amount of gold it would be necessary to throw away a corresponding amount of other stuff that was absolutely needed for the maintenance of life itself.

Since Stewart could not take any great amount of the sand along with him, he decided to take what he considered a representative sample rather than to select the richest portions. Unobtrusively, so as not to attract the attention of the men in camp, he scooped a few handfuls of the sand into his pouch and immediately went over to his mount and put it in his saddle bags.

Several months later Stewart took this sample to an assayer in Sacramento, California, to have it assayed. Not only did the man assay the sand, but he also paid the surprised captain $82 in cash for it. And to quote the captain's own words, "There wasn't an ounce over two pounds of sand in the whole sample."

When Garcia saw Stewart gather a sample of the sand to take along, he decided to do the same thing. So while the men were engaged in loading the pack on the mule after dinner, he slipped down to the creek and got some of the dirt for himself. He didn't have a leather pouch to put it it, so he gathered some of the broad leaves from a "skunk cabbage" plant growing nearby and put his gold in them; then he wrapped his handkerchief around the bundle and tied it securely.

How much sand Garcia got is not known, but it could not have been much—not as much as Stewart had taken—but it was enough to net him $47 in cash when he sold it in California a short time later. This was Garcia's own statement.

Stewart and his party had not traveled over a couple of hundred yards into the timber over the low ridge back of their noonday camp, when the captain, who was in the lead, discovered fresh moccasin tracks in the soft earth! The tracks were pointed in the opposite direction from which the Stewart party was traveling. Apparently one lone Indian, a youth, had passed by there so recently that "his tracks were so fresh they were still smoking." That meant that there were Indians, possibly an encampment, somewhere in the vicinity. This discovery caused the captain some consternation and a lot of uneasiness. He halted briefly, called his men's attention to the tracks, and said: "Boys, there are more Indians some place around here. Apparently only one Indian made these tracks. Maybe he was a scout, but wherever there is one Indian there is sure to be a lot more nearby. We must be on our guard, and be ready for a fight any minute; and we got to travel fast."

They traveled as fast as the nature of the rough terrain would permit. Only one minor mishap caused them any delay. They had some trouble with a couple of their packs on a rocky hillside, and had to stop long enough to reload them on the mules. Stewart's horse had cast a shoe earlier in the afternoon, so, while the men were adjusting the packs on the mules, the captain got a shoeing outfit and replaced the shoe on his mount. He laid the tools—a shoeing hammer, rasp, and clenching iron—in a small recess in a ledge of rock, while he helped the men with one of the mules that was "kicking up quite a fuss." In the excitement the tools were forgotten and left there. (Years later Captain Stewart would see that shoeing outfit again.)

The rest of the trip to California was uneventful so far as this story is concerned. At Sacramento Garcia left the party, marketed his gold as earlier noted, found employment there as a vaquero, and remained in the golden state for many years. He saw no more of Stewart nor Stewart of him while on the coast.

For various and valid reasons Captain Stewart did not return immediately to the San Juan country to exploit his rich discovery. He was in the army at the time, so was not at liberty to go back until his term of enlistment expired. He was a young man who enjoyed activity and adventure. In California at the time he found both. He was a practical man, not a dreamer. He fully appreciated the difficulties and danger that would be encountered in trying to do anything with his placer in the wild and uncharted

154

San Juan country, dominated at that period by hostile Utes. After he was mustered out of army service, he got a government contract of carrying the mail which he held for many years; and he engaged in a number of other activities that gave him both profit and adventure. He was making money and having an interesting time in doing it, both of which circumstances mitigated his urge to return to his rich discovery. But he always remembered his "find" back in the San Juan country and intended to return to it when conditions warranted. Like many other men who figure they have a sure thing, Stewart figured he could return and garner the wealth from his bonanza in later years when he was too old to engage in other and more competitive undertakings. He was a discreet man, however, and held his own counsel about his discovery. He figured he was the only man who actually knew where it was or how rich it was. He knew the Mexican youth had seen the sands, but he did not think the lad would remember anything about it. At least if he did, he would not know how valuable it was.

Stewart didn't know that the boy had imitated his example and had taken a sample of the sand.

By the early Seventies the Utes in southwestern Colorado had been forcibly subdued, and the first permanent white settlers had begun to establish themselves in the San Juan region. By the Eighties it was safe for a white man to travel alone and carry on his activities in remote and isolated parts of the country.

It was at this period that Captain Stewart returned to the area to lead a life of semi-retirement and to hunt his fabulous "find" of thirty odd years before.

He had been thrifty in the days of his prosperity in California and had saved up a neat little financial stake. He bought a farm near Chama, New Mexico, a thriving railroad and lumber town on the recently constructed D&RG Railroad, and about forty miles southeast of the Pagosa Hot Springs. Stewart had traveled across the very spot in which this town was located when he and his men had gone up the Little Chama on their trip many years before.

With this farm as a home and headquarters, Stewart quietly and unobtrusively began his quest. He had no illusions about the simplicity of his task. He knew that, after the lapse of so many years since he had traveled through this country, he could not hope to follow his former trail and unerringly go directly to his treasure. He would need to familiarize himself again with the whole terrain and systematically work out the course he had followed then. But he had no doubts or misgivings about ultimate success in his enterprise. He was more certain of it in fact after his first exploratory trip to the Pagosa Hot Springs where he took the bath that he had planned to have there more than thirty years before.

He confided the purpose of his mission to no one. For three successive summers he diligently carried on his quest by himself. As soon as the snow would melt sufficiently in the spring to permit him to get about in the high mountains, he would be off, and he would continue to make frequent trips from then until the snow came again to shut him out in the fall; and always he went in the same direction—northwest from Pagosa Springs.

During these years Stewart became well and widely known all over the eastern part of the San Juan basin by the affectionate title of "Uncle Stewart." He was an old man now past sixty years of age and wore a long white beard which was always meticulously clean and neatly trimmed. He was still agile, active, and "spry as a kitten." He was still tall and slender but carried himself erect with shoulderd "squared back like all other good military men" of that period. And he was still an expert horseman. His favorite mount was a powerful, iron-gray horse of good bottom and plenty of vitality.

So far as Stewart knew there was not a person in the country who had seen him in years gone by, or that knew his secret. But the captain didn't know that the same keen Indian eyes that had seen him when he discovered his gold many years before had seen and had recognized him now. True, he was changed some in physical appearance by the passage of time—but an Indian never forgets, and never talks. He could have told Stewart some very startling information—but he didn't talk. There were still many older Utes in the country who had been living there when Stewart made his first trip through the district. Among these were Tallion, Palon—so named because he had a bald spot on his head, something unusual among Indians—Narizon—so called because he had an uncommonly big nose—and Gregorio, a leathery and wrinkled old patriarch of the tribe. The Indians knew why Stewart made his trips back into the high mountains; they knew what he was hunting for. To them his missions were no secret. The Indians didn't need to be told what he was after. They already knew. Because Stewart had a long, white, beard, the Utes named him "White Whiskers." So far as the white settlers were concerned, they neither knew nor cared about Captain Stewart's trips. It was nothing uncommon for a man to be riding alone in the back country in those days, and it was considered bad manners for anyone to ask questions about a man's mission when he was out alone. So, for three successive summers, Stewart made his solitary trips of exploration in the mountains. At least he thought these trips were solitary, and so far as was known for many years, they were. The Indians knew differently. They "shadowed" Stewart on all of his earlier trips. They knew where he went, and what he did while he was out.

The Utes had been subdued and had been assigned to a reservation which was one of the most absurd and "cockeyed" affairs in all of the federal government's dealings with the Indians. This reservation was a narrow strip of land lying east-west along the Colorado-New Mexico state line, but did not include any of the mountain or foothill country so dear to the Ute tribe. The Indians were supposed to remain on this reservation, and while on it were supposed to be free from molestation from the white men. Neither one of these conditions was kept. The reservation was poorly and inefficiently policed. There were violations of the terms of the Brunot Treaty with the Utes by both the white men and the Indians, which fanned the fire of hatred the Utes had for the Whites.

The Utes were less culpable in their violations than were the white men. It was hard for them to stay on this narrow strip of land and remain cut off from the adjacent areas to the north, which for generations past had been their undisputed possession and their favorite hunting grounds. They considered the white men an intruder and an interloper in this domain, and they hated him bitterly for it. They would frequently slip away from the

157

reservation and indulge in the happy adventure of roving and hunting over this delightful country as was their unrestricted custom in former years. So long as they remained in the "back country," in the hills away from white settlements, they were not molested by the white men, and mostly they kept out of the white man's sight.

The older Indians, like Tallian, Palon, Narizon, and many others, knew the whole country like a boy knows his own back yard. They knew every trail, every cutoff, and every nook and corner in the mountains. No white man in the San Juan country ever knew the mountains in such detail as these Indians did. It was this intimate knowledge of the country that made it possible for the Utes to "shadow" Stewart and yet never be detected in doing it. It was many years after Stewart's death before any knowledge of these secret Indian trips of "shadowing" him became known; but that is the Indian story which we will get to later.

After three summers of fruitless search by himself for his lost placer, Stewart confided his secret to some of the responsible stockmen of the region. All of these men were reliable fellows who would not be easily stampeded by stories of lost treasures. They were practical men, successful in their own businesses, and they did not engage in any project unless that project was reasonable and had a good foundation for success. They were the more substantial men in the community. They were "rugged individualists" and a hardy lot; otherwise they would not have been among the first settlers on a frontier. But when they became convinced that an undertaking was worthy and had a good chance of "paying off" they were willing to take a chance and do their best to make the proposition a success.

In enlisting the interest and the help of these men in the quest for his lost placer, Stewart thought that their experience in the out-of-doors, and their knowledge of the mountain country, would be of great value in the search and might well be the essential factors for success where he, alone, had failed. He didn't do it to obtain money. He didn't want any of their money, other than for them to share the modest expense of the trip if they wished to do so voluntarily. He made no big promises to them nor did he tell them any fantastic yarn about the treasure. He recited a straightforward, simple account of how and why of his lost treasure; and these men believed his story, and they continued to believe it as long as they lived.

The late Charles Stolstiemer, prominent stockman of the region, accompanied Stewart on many of these trips and helped in every way he could in the search for the lost placer. He continued to hunt for it on his own initiative for many years after Captain Stewart died. The fact that he didn't find it never shook his belief in its existence, nor mitigated his curiosity about what had happened to hide the spot so effectively. The Utes could have given him the explanation. Until the time of Stolstiemer's death in April, 1941, he firmly believed in the existence of the Stewart placer and that some future day it would be rediscovered.

Dave Mueller, an old-timer in the San Juan country, was another companion of Stewart's on many of his trips in the golden search. On one of these trips far back in the mountains somewhere near the headwaters of Pine river, Mueller and Stewart were climbing up a rough, rocky mountain side, when they paused to let their horses rest. Mueller was in the lead. He saw an old, rusted shoeing outfit lying on a protected little ledge of rock.

"Someone has been here ahead of us," he said to Stewart, as he called the latter's attention to the old tools.

"Yes. And I was that someone," replied Stewart. "I forgot those tools there on the trip through this country when I found the gold." And he recounted to Mueller the circumstances under which the shoeing outfit had been left.

"The placer," continued Stewart, "is somewhere back down that way. I found the gold quite a while before I left that shoeing outfit."

Dave Mueller passed on many years ago, but to the time he died he never doubted in the least Stewart's story, or the existence of the placer. He always believed that it would be uncovered again some day. Its rediscovery he thought was merely a matter of being at the right place at the right time to see the gold before it worked down into the sand out of sight again.

Many suggestions were made to Captain Stewart about the possible location of the placer in other parts of the mountains, and many theories were advanced as to how it had been covered by a landslide or the course of the little creek had been changed and the former water course had been filled with debris. His reply to all of these conclusions is best summed up in his own words:

"There may be placer gold in other parts of these mountains, but if there is, it is another placer. It is not the one I am hunting for. I found that gold on my way through here when I was going to California and I was traveling the most direct route I could. I was not lost either. That placer is somewhere along that route about a day and a half's travel from the Pagosa Hot Springs. It is in a little valley high up in the mountains, near the crest of the range. It is neither covered up by a landslide, nor has it washed away. The topography of the country was such that neither one of these things would happen there. The slope of the adjacent mountain side wasn't steep enough to cause a landslide. And the hillside was so well covered with vegetation that it would not wash; nor has that little brook changed its course. It was only a small stream that had its source in a big spring at the foot of the mountain slope and it flowed directly away from the hillside through a level, grassy meadow. There were no high banks on either side of it to cave in or to obstruct it. I do recall that there was a little waterfall in the main creek, of which this one was a tributary, a short distance below where we camped. But the water cascaded down over a solid rock ledge there and would never wash it away. I don't know what has happened to hide that placer, but I do know that it was not covered by a landslide, that it was not washed away, or that the creek changed its course."

Had Captain Stewart known the Indians' story he would have had the solution to the mystery shrouding his rich treasure. And very probably would have found it again.

It was many years after Stewart's death before any of the old Utes told the Indian story about the placer. They did not tell it to the white men even then. They still hated the whites too bitterly to reveal any confidences to them. However, the passage of time did assuage their bitterness to some extent, and the older Utes became friendly with several Mexican sheepmen in the region. The Mexicans treated the Indians well, became friendly with them, and often shared the hospitality of their campfire.

Here is the Indian story as related by old Tallian himself to a Mexican friend of his, Silviano Archuleta, who lives near Ignacio, Colorado. The story, translated into proper English, is told in the first person just as Tallian related it.

"Before the white men came and took this country away from us, it was the custom of my people to return to the Land of the Healing Waters (Pagosa Hot Springs) as early in the springtime as the snow would permit. In this beautiful land of pine timber, abundant grass and open spaces, hunting and fishing were always better than in the lowlands where we had our winter homes. During the season of the Long Sun (the month of June) my clan would always climb up to the cumbre (crest or summit) of the high mountains to gather medicinal roots and herbs whose curative powers were always greatest at this season. One year many Indians went up together, and we made one big camp in the edge of the timber just beyond the top of the Sagholue (Divider of Waters). I was just a moseton (a youth between the ages of twelve and sixteen years), but I was permitted to go on hunting trips in the nearby area by myself, and I had a rifle of my own. One day as I was returning along a timbered ridge to my camp I saw a small party of white men come over the top of the ridge on the opposite side of the valley, and descend down into it. I hid myself behind some rocks so I could watch them without being seen. They stopped by a big tree on the edge of the valley, not far from where I was and began to unpack their animals. They did not know I was watching them. I intended to wait until they had all of their mules unloaded, then I was going to shoot one or more of the men before I left there to notify my people. To my surprise the men only unloaded one pack animal. I knew by that act that they were only going to stop there for their dinner, so instead of shooting at them, I decided to wait and watch them, and to see what direction they went when they left. There were five white men and one Noki Yazzi (Mexican youth) in the party.

"The Noki took a bucket and went down to a little creek close by to get some water. After he dipped up the water he reached down with one hand and gathered some dirt from the bottom of the stream. He showed this to one of the men at the camp who looked at it very hard, and then went down to the creek himself.

This sitsi (older man) got some of the sand out of the creek bottom and put it in a little sack which he put in his maletta (saddle bag).

"I thought their actions were strange so as soon as the men got on their way, I hastened on to my own camp to report what I had seen. That night the Indians held a council. Some of them wanted to go overtake the white men and kill them, but it was decided not to do this because there were only a few Indian men in our camp. But the sitsies (older men) of our group determined to go and see the place where the white men had camped and to figure out why they had taken some of the dirt with them.

"'I believe,' said an old Indian, 'that they found some Bechindy Pesch (Devil Metal, the Indian name for gold) in that stream. If they did we must do something about it, because they will sure come back after more and cause us a lot of trouble.'

"I was startled when I heard this talk because we had heard how much trouble had come to other tribes when the white men found bechindy pesch in their land. I was sorry then that I had not shot some of those men the day before. Had I killed one or two of them our men would have followed up and killed the others.

"The following day I went with the sitsies to show them the place, and sure enough there was bechindy pesch in that creek. Much of it. So much that the bottom of the stream looked yellow and the Indians named the place Postuiwit (the place of the yellow dirt).

"What to do about it was our problem. Messengers were sent to call sitsies from other Ute camps to come to a council. Many came and the council was held at our camp. It was decided that the best thing to do was to cover the gold up by filling the little stream-bed with dirt and letting the water run over the top of it.

"According, this was done. The first time, we just gathered ordinary earth in our blankets and poured it in the creek until the bottom was well covered and no speck of bechindy pesch could be seen; but this dirt washed out in a short time leaving only the little rocks that were in it, and they were not enough to cover up the gold. So another council was held and at this one it was decided to fill the creek bed with logs first and then to put

162

the same kind of soil over them as grew on the banks of the creek. We did this, and soon the grass took roots and grew and this place looked like all of the rest of the meadow. No one could discern that there had ever been a stream there. Our work did not wash away that time because the water could follow along the cracks between the logs. And we fixed it where the water did come out to look just like a natural spring.

"That is the reason," concluded old Tallian with much satisfaction, "that 'White Whiskers' couldn't find the place again. He went by it many times."

A short time before he died old Palon told the same story to a Mexican friend of his, the late Benito Martinez, Sr., of Dyke, Colorado, only his account of the events was more brief and to the point. It was sufficiently vivid, however, and his description of the country was complete enough to lead the Mexican to believe he could find the place.

Benito Martinez, acting on the information given him by old Palon, searched intermittently for the placer for several years. He did not find it, but he did find old signs and indications of a Ute camp where Palon told him the old camp had been located. Benny passed on a few years ago, but always, up to the time of his death, he was sure that he would find "El Placer del Vaquero por el ano que viene (next year)." The older Mexicans in the district always refer to the "Stewart Placer" as "El placer del Vaquero" because Garcia, as previously pointed out, had returned to the country and had made a few unsuccessful trips into the mountains in quest of the golden treasure. He wanted to join with Stewart in the search, but Stewart remained aloof from the Mexican. He would have nothing in common with him. Why? No one knows.

Garcia gave up the search after Stewart refused to join with him. In a characteristic Mexican way, Garcia said that it was not the will of God for either one of them to find the lost placer because there was envy between them.

The Stewart Placer has been hunted for by all sorts of men in all sorts of places in the San Juan country all the way from the clay hill in the coal mining district around Monero on the south to the headwaters of the Rio Grande on the north; and all kinds of stories and legends have grown up concerning that famous lost treasure. Many of these tales are wild and impossible, but are recounted as being the "gospel truth" by their narrators. These yarns are all a part of the Stewart Placer story and an inseparable part of the rich treasure trove of the San Juan. They are told around the campfires or any other place where riders of the range and out-of-doors men get together.

One story relates that Stewart was a captain of cavalry in a regiment of soldiers fighting Indians in the San Juan country. He was assigned to guard duty one night to herd the company's horses. While making his rounds of the meadow in which the horses were grazing, Stewart noticed some black sands in a little creek. He dismounted and, using his hat for a gold pan, washed out some of the black sands for a sample. Then he put this sample in an envelope, tucked the envelope away among some other papers in his trunk, and forgot all about the whole occurrence. Several years later he was rummaging through his trunk for some other papers when he accidentally ran across the sample of black sands. During the interim he had gone to California, had been mustered out of the service, and was engaged in private activities. After considerable cogitating he remembered how he had come to get the sample. Then, to satisfy his curiosity, he took the sand to an assayer in Sacramento to have it assayed. He was surprised to find out that the sample was rich in gold. As soon as he could wind up his affairs in California, he came back to the San Juan country to search for the place, but he could never find it.

This story ignores some pertinent facts. A captain in the cavalry would not be assigned to ordinary guard duty; a military hat would not work as a gold pan; no man would pan gold after dark; and having panned out a sample, no man would forget all about it.

Another Placer yarn follows:

Stewart was a captain of cavalry in a regiment on military duty in the San Juan country. In a fight with the Indians, Stewart and a squad of men got cut off from the rest of the regiment by the Indians and had to make a run for their lives. In their flight they headed into the mountains northwest of Pagosa Springs. They intended to circle around the Indians, through these mountains, and arrive at Fort Lewis, a military post a few miles west of Durango.

Somewhere in their wanderings through the hills, they ran onto a shallow little rivulet that had a lot of coarse gold and nuggets on its sandy bottom. The men became so excited about the gold that they emptied the smoking tobacco out of their Bull Durham tobacco sacks in order to have something to carry their nuggets in. Finally the party found the way out of the mountains and got to Durango, where one of the soldiers was so famished for a smoke he traded a sack of the nuggets to a merchant for a sack of Bull Durham cigarette tobacco. The merchant was so impressed with the beauty and the uniformity of the nuggets that he had them strung together for a watch chain, which he, ironically enough, referred to as his string of "Golden Grains."

Years later, this story goes on to relate, Captain Stewart got out of the army and came back to the San Juan country to search for the gold. But he was so confused about the location he could never find it again. Strangely enough the story never mentions anything more about the soldiers who shared with Stewart in this fabulous discovery; nor does it take into account that there was no Durango, or Fort Lewis military post, in the San Juan basin at that period of history.

"New and strictly secret information" about the Stewart Placer was the basis for an expedition of a searching party into the clay foothills around Monero in the 1930's. The party was headed by Pete Olson, a mining man of Durango.

According to this story: The Stewart Placer had never been found because everyone had been hunting for it in the wrong part of the country. Misinformation about the route Stewart had taken when he found the gold had led men to hunt for the placer in the mountains northwest of Pagosa Springs—a section of country through which Stewart and his party did not pass. This "new and secret" information ("strictly confidential") said that Stewart was following the old Escalante trail, and that instead of going on northwest into the mountains, he turned west on the Escalante route near the headwaters of the Little Chama river, crossed over the Continental Divide onto a tributary of the San Juan and was following that dry water course down to the main stream when he found the gold. Intensive research, Olson insisted, had proven this account to be "the gospel truth." He and his party were on the "right track just as sure as God made little apples."

This story goes on: Several miles down this dry creek, the party camped under a big pine tree in a grassy flat on the bank of the wash to prepare their dinner. Stewart, captain of the party, took a shovel off a pack and went down to the stream bed to dig for camp water. He was under a high bank out of sight of the men.

He found water after the first few spades of sand. Then he started to deepen the hole a little bit, and the first shovel of sand he got was almost half gold! Stewart was so excited by his discovery, and was so afraid his men might see what had happened, that he hastily stuffed a handful of the wet sand into his pocket, filled up the hole, went back to the camp and ordered the men to reload the mules, and the party proceeded on its way without any dinner.

The soldiers were pretty much provoked by this unreasonable and arbitrary action of the captain; so when the party camped early that afternoon, several miles farther on, on the banks of the swift-flowing San Juan river, one of the soldiers gave vent to his gripe by writing a letter home.

It was this letter that contained the "new and secret information."

In it the soldier had given detailed information about the route the party had traveled, a minute description of the place where they had stopped for dinner, what had occurred there as the soldier saw it, and how the "tyrant of a damn fool captain we had made us move on without dinner." The soldier went on in the letter to describe their campsite on the San Juan in such detail that the spot could be readily recognized by anyone who had read the letter carefully, and had then hunted for the place. Olsen and his associates located this spot and proceeded from there with their search.

The soldier's letter, Olson insisted, was authentic. It had only recently been discovered by one of his associates among the possessions of a descendent of the soldier. This descendent was an itinerant mechanic. He didn't know the vital secret of the letter but had kept the epistle merely as a keepsake. The descendent knew nothing about the Stewart Placer but Olson and his associates did, hence they recognized the valuable information the letter contained. The descendent of the soldier, however, didn't want to part with the letter—it had such a high sentimental value for him. But, finally, after much persuasion, Olson and his group succeeded in substituting $150 in cash for the "sentimental value" of the letter and both they and the "descendent" were well pleased with the trade.

The Olson party spent the greater part of one summer in the Monero area hunting for the famous placer. They followed the descriptions given in the letter, although they found them mighty vague when they got out in the district and tried to apply them. They panned every dry wash and arroya in the area without so much as getting a color.

Either their information was not as sure as they thought it was, or God never made little apples, because they never found the gold.

Meanwhile the descendent left the country and was never seen by any of them again. Maybe it was true that he knew nothing about the Stewart Placer, but, if it was, he succeeded, nevertheless, in getting $150 in cash for his "ignorance."

Another old-timer in the San Juan country, a long-time resident of Pagosa Springs, we will call Stanton, considers himself an authority on the Stewart Placer. For many years he has steeped himself in the lore of that fabulous lost treasure. He, himself, admits that he has given the matter "deep and analytical thought" for many years, and it is his "considerate opinion, after duly weighing all available information in connection with Stewart's own account of the incidents; and the subsequent unsuccessful attempts to find the placer, that the place is off the 'beaten path' where other men have searched. It is on Quen Sabe mountain." And on that low, dry, grassy, table-topped foothill, located a few hours ride north of Pagosa Springs, he has spent a great deal of time in fruitless search.

"It stands to reason, don't it?" Stanton points out. "They hain't found the placer no place else, but they hain't no body but me ever looked fer it on Quen Sabe mountain. But sure as shootin' that's whar it be. When Stewart and his sojers circled around Pagosa Springs to dodge the Injuns, they went ferther north than they thought they did, and crossed Quen Sabe. I figger that's whar they found the gold but they got all mixed up in tellin' about it so many years later. Stewart always said he seed a waterfall clost by his placer. Wal' sir, from the top of Quen Sabe yu'ken see the falls on Four Mile Crick over by Pagosa Peak. And them are some falls. No man would soon fergit 'em. I know the falls are not on Quen Sabe, they are two mile northwest of it, but that don't make no difference, they are thar just the same. And as I said afore, Stewart musta got mixed up some in his rememberin'."

So, whenever there is a grubstake available, Stanton hies himself up to Quen Sabe to camp. After all, it is a nice place for an outing, easily accessible, good hunting in season, plenty of grass, and a pleasant place to be. If you are going to hunt for a lost treasure, why not choose a delightful place to do it in?

It remained for George W. Oprey to introduce a new and refreshing element into the quest for the Stewart Placer. Oprey's whole idea was comprehensive and different, very different, from anything that had ever been heard of before.

Oprey was a stout, stocky man of medium height, wrote a good hand, and had a fair education. He posed as a professional prospector and claimed to be an "original" geologist. He qualified on both counts: As a prospector, his "pay streak" was on top of the ground, and it made no difference to him whose pocket that pay streak came out of—old maid school teachers, honest farmers, or gullible, professional men, they were all the same to Oprey. He staked mining claims all over the country but never did a "lick of work" on any of them; and his explanations of the geology of the district were certainly original—very original. Oprey showed up in the San Juan mountains along the Continental Divide around the upper reaches of the Rio Grande, in the middle Thirties. Where he came from, Oprey alone knew. He used the famous mining town of Creede as a base from which to operate. He established a series of camps, supply stations he called them, high up near timberline for sixty miles along the Rio Grande side of the Continental Divide—from Spar City to Beartown. He had no pack stock of his own with which to transport his supplies back into the mountains, so he solved his problem by the simple expedient of inducing men who did have to pack his stuff in there for him. In return for this service Oprey would "stake in" these fellows on some of the "really rich discoveries" he was going to make. And those discoveries would be made "just as soon as I can complete an analytical study of the original geology of this fabulous domain." Oprey always referred to his study as being of the original geology but never as being an original study; and always the whole country was a fabulous domain. Oprey never seemed to have any difficulty in obtaining packers.

Oprey, in fact, was mighty generous in his "staking in" other persons on the "truly wonderful" mining claims he would discover. All anyone had to do to "get in" on them, was to put up a "grub-stake," and a minor sum that, he pointed out, would be an infinitesimally small amount when compared to the stupendous returns that could be had from just one rich "discovery." And with his new approach, his fresh and different concept of the geology of the "domain," Oprey was going to make, not just one "rich discovery," but many.

Oprey seemed to have had a "good line," because he always had plenty of grubstakes.

With a few days' supply of food, a frying pan, a coffee pot, a prospector's pick, and other accessories, including a generous number of printed mining claim location forms, Oprey prowled around through the mountains adjacent to his "supply stations." This was his method, he said, of making his "analytical study of the original geology of the fabulous domain."

In making his study of the region, it was only logical that Oprey would visit the operating mines in the area—at Beartown, at Creede, and at Spar City, and would obtain specimens, especially high grade ones, of their ore. These specimens, he insisted, were only for study and comparison in order to further his knowledge of the region. It seems he collected a lot of rich specimens.

If Oprey ever got these choice pieces of rich ore "confused" with the samples he took from any of the numerous mining claims he staked, no one knew it but himself—and he was not telling. He must have taken lots of samples because he always had a number of assay sheets made in triplicate, on hand, and everyone of those assay returns showed high values.

And he must have located lots of claims. He had location notices tacked on stakes all over the district. Oprey's name, followed by that of one or two other people, always appeared as locators on these notices. Oprey always filled out these printed forms in duplicate or triplicate, depending on the number of names put on the location stake, and he would send these extra copies to the other persons whose names were on the stake, as proof to them that they were being "staken in" on mining claims in return for their grubstake, just as Oprey had told them he would do. As a further proof of his integrity Oprey always mentioned to these "partners" that he, himself, had not filed the location notice with the county recorder, but left that task entirely up to his partners so they would know by making the filing themselves, that their interest in that said claim was a matter of public record. Incidently this arrangement saved Oprey the filing fee.

Along with the completed location notices Oprey sent to his "grubstakers" he always enclosed an assay sheet that showed high values of a sample of ore which he said was taken from a vein in the vicinity. It was highly probable, he always pointed out, that this same vein transversed this particular claim, but it would require further research to determine its precise location—and, of course, additional "research" called for additional grubstake money. He usually got it.

Just what Oprey meant by "additional research" seems rather vague. It didn't mean anything requiring hard, manual labor, like digging a deeper shaft or a longer tunnel, because Oprey never so much as stuck a pick in the ground on any of his claims. It was always so much easier, so much more interesting, for him, to move on over the next mountain to hunt for a better vein there.

The Stewart Placer was really the project he was interested in, Oprey confidentially confessed to a campfire companion one July evening high up on the Continental Divide at the head of the Middle Fork. That fabulous treasure was the biggest thing in the whole San Juan country, Oprey said, and it had been intensively hunted for by many different men over a long period of years; but all of these fellows were searching in the wrong part of the country; and they all lacked the proper geological knowledge to hunt for that treasure intelligently. Now he, Oprey, had the real, true information about that famous Placer, and he had an authentic map showing its approximate location. The Stewart Placer was down on the Rio Grande river! But let us loaf around the campfire and listen while Oprey tells his own story:

"I got my map and my information about the Stewart Placer direct from the Gonzales family in Abiquiu (New Mexico). Their grandfather was the cook in Kit Carson's camp up here on the Rio Grande above the Five-Mile Crossing, when Captain Stewart and four other soldiers came to the camp. Carson was trapping furs up here that summer, and Stewart and his men were scouting out a route for a transcontinental railroad. They stayed in Carson's camp several days and scouted from there back to the Continental Divide, hunting for a pass to run the railroad through.

"About midafternoon one day, when everyone was gone from the camp except Gonzales, he saw Captain Stewart, all alone, riding across the meadow on the opposite bank of the river. When Stewart crossed a long, shallow, finger of water that extended back from the river for some distance into the meadow, he suddenly pulled his horse to a halt, dismounted, hastily investigated the sand in the bottom of the inlet. Then Stewart did what Gonzales thought was a very strange thing. He pulled off his big sombrero, filled it with sand from the creek bed, and washed that sand around and around in his hat. Apparently he finally got tired of such child's play and emptied the rest of the sand from his hat into a leather pouch, and put the pouch into his saddle bag.

"Right then and right there Stewart discovered his placer.

"Grandfather Gonzales knew nothing about panning gold, so Stewart's actions seemed so odd to him they left a deep impression on his mind. Also Grandfather Gonzales was quite an artist. He like to draw and spent some of his leisure time drawing detailed maps of the immediate area around his camp. He had, just that morning, finished an excellent map of this particular camp area. On it he had shown a big, graceful curve the river made through the meadows of the bottom land, he had shaded in the banks of the stream, outlined the meadows, even to the extent of showing the slender inlet where Stewart played in the sand, and indicated the mountains and the trees along the sides of the valley. A fine map, indeed, drawn in detail right on the spot. Stewart's peculiar

171

act so impressed Gonzales that he immediately marked that very spot on his map and saved the map to show to his children when he got home and told them about the Americano's funny antics. And that is the map I got. I'll show it to you, so you can judge for yourself."

Oprey pulled a waterproofed wallet out of an inside pocket and from it extracted a sheet of paper that was a bit frayed around the edges and had begun to turn a pale yellow, either from age or from too much sunlight. He spread it out on the ground in the firelight and, apparently with absolute sincerity, said, "Take a look at the only authentic map of the Stewart Placer. That map is older than you or me. Ain't it?"

"It looks pretty old," replied his companion without committing himself any further. He recognized the type of paper the map was drawn on, and he knew that that particular class of paper had not been manufactured prior to 1895—43 years after Stewart found his placer, and 27 years after the death of Kit Carson in 1868. Grandfather Gonzales must have drawn his map with a mighty long pencil of time.

"I figured that the Gonzales family hadn't ever heard about the Stewart Placer, so they didn't know what an important document this map was. I did. So I started in to get possession of it. Gonzaleses didn't want to part with it because it was a sort of keepsake, but I finally got it from them for $50. They wanted $100 to begin with and I had a hard time to get them down to half price. Even then, they seemed hesitant to part with it for five of my ten spots, and I never felt sure about the deal until I had possession of the map, and Gonzales had the money." Maybe the Gonzaleses felt the same way about the trade, thought Oprey's campfire companion, but he made no comment.

"Now, I have been making a study of this high country along the divide, and my conclusions prove this map is right. There has been a lot of geological action in these mountains in past ages.

"First, there were the glaciers that came down from Alaska and covered all of this country at one time. Marks left by this glacial action can still be seen in different spots in these mountains. I've found several of them. Some of these glaciers had lots of gold frozen in them—coarse gold and nuggets. And that was what Stewart found—glacial gold.

"Then, before these glaciers had melted, the volcanic age came along. This district was a great volcanic area at that time. All these mountain peaks around here are extinct volcanoes. In daylight seven of them can be seen from this very spot. The Red Mountain back here on the head of the Piedra was one of them— the last one. That is how it got its red color because of the intense heat that burned its rocks red like a brick burned in a kiln. Of course, the professional geologists claim that iron oxide in the rock is what gives them that red color, but that is where the geologists are wrong. It was the heat, and I know because I have studied all of this geology up here in the original. I have not depended on books for my information.

"Well sir, when all those volcanoes got to going they made this country pretty hot, and that caused the glaciers to melt and to break up mighty fast. Big chunks of them broke loose in some of these 'rincones' up along the divide, and floated down into the Rio Grande valley before they could melt. That is how the gold Stewart found got down there where he found it. It was in one of those big chunks of ice that broke loose from up here; and I have studied the country enough so that I know just what cove that iceberg came out of.

"That 'berg' was big enough that when it got down into the Rio Grande valley where the water spread out, it lodged on the bottom of the river and choked up the channel. The water had to find a new way around it, and that's how the big curve happened in the river—the big curve that Gonzales showed on his map. That big chunk of ice melted right there and left all that glacial gold on that spot.

"Of course as time went by vegetation began to grow over the place, and to cover up the gold. That little inlet where Stewart found the gold just hadn't had time to grow over yet. But it is growed over now except for a small indentation right at the edge of the main river. And I know exactly where that one is. Before another season ends I'll have the Stewart Placer.

"And I am not staking in anybody else with me on it either.

I've worked its discovery out myself, so I am going to harvest all the benefit."

Apparently the end of that "another" season mentioned by Oprey has never come. At least he has never found the lost Stewart Placer, and if he is still hunting for it, he is doing it in whatever other realm he went to after he departed from this one. Considering Oprey's "shady" methods of acquiring grubstakes, it has been suggested he would need asbestos tools for any searching he might be making now. He died a few years ago.

Like many other yarns about the Stewart Placer, Oprey's story was a mixture of fact and fancy woven together on the elastic fabric of imagination.

There are two classes of treasure hunters—the practical, analytical kind who must have sound reasons to interest them in a lost treasure, and then only in a specific one; and the ordinary treasure seekers. The majority of men belong in the latter class.

The ordinary run of treasure hunters are dreamers. They are a fanciful lot who have a flagrant disregard for fact and for logic. They may be sensible in other activities of life, but in seeking treasure they mentally fall into the realm of fancy and blithely pursue its pleasant paths. They never reason to a conclusion but rather conjure up a conclusion that fits their dreams and then arrange reasons to support it.

Oprey's story conformed to the regular pattern. Maybe the Gonzales family knew more about the Stewart Placer than he credited them for. To say the least, they cashed in for $50 on it in exchange for an "original" map drawn on a type of paper that did not exist at the time it was supposed to be drawn, and a map to which Oprey's imagination ascribed the vital details that gave it valuable.

In a similar fanciful vein Oprey's narrative made use of some facts, conveniently misarranged, to impart an atmosphere of reality to the yarn. Kit Carson was a famous scout and trapper of the west contemporaneous with Stewart. In previous years he had trapped on the headwaters of the Rio Grande but had quit all trapping prior to the Mexican War. At the time Stewart found his placer Carson was living at Taos, also an Indian Pueblo and trading center 200 miles away. No trapping was ever done by

174

anyone during the summer. The furs were no good during that season of the year.

True enough, an expedition hunting for a railroad passage through the mountains made a trip up the Rio Grande during that period of history; but that expedition was a private affair, not military, in charge of General John C. Fremont representing Senator Benton of Missouri and his associates. The trip was made in November, 1845—not June 1852—and Carson was in Taos at that time. Also there are ample indications of both volcanic and glacial actions in the San Juan mountains but just how such natural forces could accomplish the outlandish and impossible feats attributed to them in Oprey's yarn is beyond the realm of reason to comprehend.

It is true that some glaciers carried gold, and that some of it has been found in the San Juan country; but that fact fails to explain how a chunk of ice so huge that it could choke a big, swift river, could slip out of a high mountain gulch, cascade down innumerable bluffs and ledges, float through narrow gorges, and yet arrive in one big piece at a spot in a river channel twenty miles away. But fanciful dreams take no account of the improbable and they blithely accept the impossible.

The conclusion was that the lost Stewart gold was there; reasons to support that conclusion had to be found. Oprey "found" them. But he did not find the Placer.

But men of flesh and blood are not the only ones who seek the lost Stewart Placer. No sir, not by any means. The older Mexicans in the region tell of a phantom rider on a phantom horse who rides the high range in the summer twilight in quest of the elusive treasure. He always goes, they will tell you, unerringly to the same little valley in the mountains where Stewart found his gold; he always rides a circular course around the meadow and unfailingly returns to a big spruce tree in the edge of the timber at the lower end of the valley, and when he rides behind that tree, horse and rider disappear. No, senor, he never rides out of sight over a ridge; he rides behind that tree and vanishes—maybe, senor, he rides right into that tree. "Pero siempre disparese." Always vanishes.

This phantom horse and rider have been seen, the Mexicans

insist, in every mountain cove, valley, and vega along the Continental Divide from the head of the Piedra to La Ventana on the head of the Pine—a distance of forty mountain miles. Which particular valley he has been seen in depends on the narrator's idea of where the Stewart Placer is located.

The rider is tall and straight, like a soldier, and has a long, white beard, and he is always in a hurry. His powerful mount, a stocky, iron-gray steed, never tires, never pauses to rest, but seems to plunge effortlessly up the steep, rocky, mountain trails with incredibly long strides. The iron shoes on his hoofs silently knock giant sparks, comparable to the blaze from a campfire, from the rocks in his path.

"Por verdad," they insist, the spirit of Captain Stewart still rides in the San Juan.

EPILOGUE

The adage that truth is stranger than fiction is merely a lame excuse that mankind makes for itself as a cover for its inability to perceive or to explain some extraordinary set of fact or circumstances whose logical relationships are not readily apparent; and just such a condition is what has made the Stewart Placer such a baffling puzzle to many people since its existence became generally known.

There is no doubt in the minds of those in position to judge the matter that the fabulous placer exists, just as Captain Stewart and El Vaquero said it did. Both of these men cashed in gold that was taken from the placer; and those men who later knew Stewart had no doubts whatsoever about his integrity. A banker, who knew Captain Stewart well and handled much of his business for him, expressed the opinion generally held by everyone in the San Juan country when he remarked: "There is no doubt about the existence of the Stewart Placer, but where?"

And that is more than a $64 question.

And having been found once, why can't it be found again? When there is no doubt about its existence, and about the area in which it was found? Why doesn't it show up on the surface of the creek bed again as it did when Stewart found it? Or why can't it be traced by panning colors along the creek bottoms until the one leading to the placer is discovered, and then, this one, richer in colors than all the rest, followed up to the source from which the colors came—which would be the lost placer. This would be the natural way, the usual way, that things should happen in the normal search for placer gold; but this series of occurrences does not happen in the case of the Stewart Placer. Why? There must be logical reasons. And there are.

The Stewart Placer is still an enigma but when it is found, as it will be some day, the reasons why it remained an enigma so long will be readily apparent—and very logical.

There are extensive marks of glacial action all along the Continental Divide in this section of the mountains. Oprey's fantastic story was correct so far as signs of glacial action were concerned. Some glaciers carried gold—in spots. Some of these spots were extensive and rich, other spots were small, only a few nuggets or coarse grains.

A little glacial gold has been found at widely separated spots along this section of the big divide, nothing big, but sufficient to prove that glacial gold exists in this area. The writer found two nuggets about as big as a pea and a few coarse grains of gold in a little crack in bedrock on the top of the divide at the head of Trout creek, where indications of glacial action were unmistakable. This gold could not have come from some point higher up, because there wasn't any place higher up. This spot was on top. And there wasn't any more gold around there either. The writer looked, Nuf said. Nacario Arragon, a friend of the writer, made a similar find, on top of the divide at the head of the Ute creek near La Ventana—forty miles farther west. And other men have made the same kind of discoveries at other spots in the area. All of these finds, while small in value, prove that the glaciers in this district carried gold along with the earth and gravel frozen in them. Some spots in those glaciers were rich in gold, and wherever that spot of ice melted in the slow process of being changed into water, the fabulous cargo of treasure would be deposited on a small area.

A deposit of gold made under these circumstances would be made independent of topography of the country, and would not depend for its existence on gold bearing veins in adjacent mountainsides. The cove where the glacier melted was a rock bound basin in which the gold settled on bedrock that was lower than the outlet of the basin—in other words, a sort of shallow lake. When the water got high enough in the basin it flowed out over the lower rim but carried no gold with it. Gradually the lake filled with earth and vegetation grew over it to form a meadow or vega, as such spots are known in the San Juan country. The little creek or side tributary in which Stewart found the gold was on the outer rim of the glacial basin where the gold laid on bedrock—that is why it had not been covered with sand. It could not sink any deeper, and what little sand that accumulated was carried away by the water. That was the reason the dirt the Indians first filled the creek bed with washed away but left the small rock and gold there.

These vegas support a luxuriant growth of moutain grass. They are, indeed, meadows with a turf or sod that is thick and tough. The grass grows heavy along the banks of the little watercourses in these meadows, and sometimes, on the smaller ones, grows clear over them forming a solid mat over the stream underneath. Any man that has been a ranger in the San Juan mountains many years has by his own observation seen this happen more times than one. Where the process happens naturally, there are always open spots here and there in the covering that admit trash and debris that will, occasionally, temporarily choke the stream up and cause it to overflow, or break the covering for a little way to relieve the pressure, but always the grass grows back again to hide the watercourse.

But in the case of the Stewart Placer the Utes left no opening to admit trash, and the logs they so ingeniously layed in the streambed provided an ample course for the water from the big spring. The logs rotted in the course of time, but their decay was a gradual process in which time the roots of the grass the Indians transplated over them replaced the wood, and the tiny channel became a permanent underground watercourse, having no surface indications to betray its existence. But some day something will happen that will cause a break in that grassy covering and will again expose the gold lining the bottom of that creek.

Fortunate will be the man who passes that way then and is curious enough to have a look.

I am keeping my glasses well polished in anticipation of another trip back into the San Juans.

The Ute Indians Dumped the Gold

Somewhere near the confluence of the Piedra river and Stolsteimer creek, south of the famous Chimney Rocks on Highway 160 in southwestern Colorado, is a little spot of ground containing the richest concentration of gold in all of the San Juan basin. There are five mule-loads of bullion in that little spot which at the current value of gold would be worth between $350,000 and $400,000—a mighty tidy little sum of cash in any man's country at any time. The Ute Indians dumped that gold there; and it was a part of the price that they exacted from five white men for a few pieces of venison and some bread stolen from an Indian camp. The balance of the price the Utes took was the lives of four of the white men and their entire outfit of horses, mules, and camp—one of the men escaped. We will hear of him later. Had the Utes gotten him also in the massacre, there would have been no story at a later date to tell the white man's side of the events and corroborate the tragic accounts of the incident as told by several different old Utes warriors, many, many years later. The old Utes told their story to old Mexican friends first, and later, to a few, a very select few, white men with whom they had become friendly in the twilight of their lives. The writer was one of these select few.

Sometime in October, 1851, or 1852, a group of five white men, with saddle horses and seven pack mules, crossed the Colorado river at the present location of the booming uranium town ⌐ Moab, Utah, and began their long trip across the San Juan country of southwestern Colorado. The men were on their way ¦ ⌐ the goldfields of California to Taos or Santa Fe, New Mexico, where they could get on the main Santa Fe Trail to make the rest of their trip back to the States in company with freighters making their return trip east.

Five of the seven mules were loaded with gold bullion—two sacks to each mule. How these five men had gotten so much gold, and why they were transporting it across country themselves through a region where there were no main trails or travel, remains a considerable mystery. Circumstances strongly indicate that they had not come by this gold legitimately and had purposely chosen this remote route the better to avoid detection.

How they came by the gold is less important than the fact that they had it.

All that is known about their journey previous to their crossing the Colorado river in southeastern Utah that October day was the brief remark made by the lone survivor years later that they had come in a circuitous way from California; but after the party had crossed the river they were in Ute Indian territory and sharp Indian eyes kept watch on this curious party of strangers as they traveled through the country. Many of the Indians had never seen a white man before, and these dark, roughly-dressed, long-haired, heavily bearded specimens of humanity were objects of intense interest to them. One man, however, was an outstanding individual in the group—he had no whiskers. He had hair on his head like the others but no whiskers on his face. The Indians were so intrigued by this curious fact they they later referred to him as "Naked Face." The importance of this allusion will be apparent later.

From the crossing of the Colorado on into the San Juan country the party of white men followed, roughly, the route traveled by Father Escalante and his party some seventy-five years before, when that intrepid priest was looking for a northern trail from Santa Fe to the missions in California. It is doubtful, however, that these white adventurers had any knowledge of Escalante and his expedition. They were simply traveling across country toward a specific goal, and took the easiest and most logical route to get there.

From the Colorado they swung out in a southeastward course in a sort of arc around the base of the high mountains—the La Sals, the La Platas, and the San Juans—and traveled along the geological trough between the mountains and the lower, sedimentary tablelands of Mesa Verde, where the famous national park of that name is located.

The party crossed the Rio de las Animas a little way below

the site of the present thriving city of Durango, and from there for some unaccountable reason they headed almost due east across Florida Mesa and the valley of the Pine river, for a notch in a range of low, rolling hills now known as the Ignacio Mountains. Their logical course would have been to have swung more to the southeast across less rugged country, to encounter the San Juan river near the present community of Allison. What capricious quirk of fate influenced them to head off their course and go to the Ignacio Mountains will never be known. They made a bad mistake.

The Ignacio Mountains are really not mountains at all, but a long, high ridge with a series of promonotories and notches along its length with little creeks, valleys, and canyons on its slopes that drain into the Pine river on the west and the Piedra on the east. It is the divide between the two watersheds.

This was a beautiful country, covered with a magnificent stand of western yellow pine, scrub oak, and native berries. It was a land of abundant grass and abundant game in the autumn of the year as the elk and the deer drifted down from the high mountains immediately north. Open parks, and beautiful little valleys along the creeks, and plenty of wood and water made this a favorite camping place and hunting ground for the Utes at this season of the year.

The main or central camp of the Ute clan that claimed this land as their home was in the valley on upper Fosset creek on the Piedra slope, where in later years Mike Pargin had a cattle ranch. However, individual families or groups of two or three families preferred to camp out to themselves, setting up their tepees near each other in some park or open, little valley.

This was the setup on that fateful October afternoon when the party of white men crossed the notch in the divide and suddenly rode smack into an Indian camp in the edge of the timber in a beautiful valley at the head of a creek that drained east into the Piedra. The white men were as surprised at this encounter as the Ute squaws and papooses in the camp were but they were not nearly so terror-stricken.

At sight of those rough-appearing, bewhiskered strangers the squaws let out a yell of terror and with their kids fled into hiding

182

in the brush and timber. Page Wright, a venerable old Ute who lived to a mighty old age on his allotment on the Pine river below the town of Ignacio, was one of the tiny Indian tots in this group. He was mighty young at that time—at most, not over five years old—but the terror of the occasion made such a lasting impression on his memory that he never forgot it. He recounted the incident with the utmost of clarity to the writer on several different occasions. There were no Indian men in the camp at the time. They were out hunting.

The white men had no intentions of doing any harm either to the squaws or to the camp. In fact they were so surprised at encountering a camp and live Indians that, temporarily, they had no intentions, period. These were the first Indians they had actually seen in the entire trip from the Colorado, and they were not mentally conditioned for the encounter. Other Indians had seen them all along the line, but they had not seen a single Redskin.

After a few minutes of hesitancy, the white men recovered from their shock and realized the precariousness of their position. The quickest way out of the dilemma, for them, was to bypass the camp and continue on their way, and had they done that they perhaps would not have been disturbed. But as they went by the small group of tepees the sight of lots of fresh meat hung out to dry, and the delicious aroma of meat left cooking on the fire by the squaws in their hasty flight, was too much of a temptation for the hungry men to resist. They had been living on short rations for several days, had been riding hard since they crossed the Colorado, and had seen no game to kill enroute.

Here was lots of meat and bread, they reasoned, and the Indian camp was deserted, no one to offer any resistence. Why not take some of the food along with them? The Indians surely should not resent such a little thing as the theft of some grub. "Naked Face" and one of the other fellows dismounted to gather the food while the other three men went on with the pack stock. It only took a few minutes to collect what food the men wanted, but it was a nervous few minutes, and when Naked Face started to mount his horse the animal became frightened and in his prancing about while being mounted, knocked one of the teepees over.

The two men attached no importance to this seemingly trivial incident. What did an upset tepee amount to, anyway? It could be set up again in a few minutes and no harm done, at least that is what the men thought. The rest of their party was already going out of sight around a bend in the valley and these fellows were in a hurry to overtake them. They rode away from the camp without so much as a backward glance. They might have been much less carefree had they known what had happened to that upset tepee and what tragic consequences were to follow in a few hours. The tepee had fallen across a campfire and the whole Indian camp was burned up as a result!

The white men continued on their way down this long draw and came out on the west bank of the Piedra river, at some point opposite the mouth of the Stolsteimer, about dusk. This long draw must have been either Turkey creek, Skull Canyon, or Goose creek because those are the three tributaries emptying into the Piedra opposite the Stolsteimer. It was while his party was traveling down this long draw that afternoon that Naked Face saw the Chimney Rocks and remembered them so well that he easily recognized them again some forty years later.

The party camped that night somewhere on the Piedra near the mouth of the Stolsteimer. Whether they camped on the east bank of the river or on the west bank, above or below the confluence of the Stolsteimer, and whether the mouth of that erratic little stream is in the same location today as it was then, has never been definitely established. Wherever the camp may have been, adjacent to it was a bank of some sort, and somewhere in the immediate vicinity, perhaps on this same bank, was a shallow, narrow ravine, a short one. These physical features are not very outstanding landmarks in that locality. There are many such banks and ravines in the area.

The white men were up early the next morning, and shortly after daylight one of the men, Naked Face, was driving the saddle horses and pack mules up to the camp to be caught and saddled, when the Utes suddenly attacked from behind the bank. Naked Face was about 200 yards from the camp when he heard

Snow Trouble with jacks, near Continental Divide.

Chimney Rock, near Pagosa Springs.
One of Craven's landmarks.

Stewart Placer area and Continental Divide.

Hidden Lake, source of Piedra River.

A prospector at home.

Stagecoach party on a treasure trail.

A prospector, searching for a lead.

Early-day prospectors, ready for Utes.

A promising prospect. Struck it rich!

Placer mine at work. Keystone Hill near Telluride, 1890.

Rush to the San Juans. Scene at Dolores, Colorado. *State Historical Society of Colorado.*

After the storm. Mountain scene from Ouray.

187

Spanish blaze high on the tree; lower, a spot blaze to indicate change of direction. On Continental Divide.

Prospect pleases—a working mine now. Note the dense forest growth making discovery of lodes difficult.

Any way to reach treasure of bullion. Take the Rio Grande Southern RR. *State Historical Society of Colorado*

Ophir, Colo., early photo. Golden Fortune on Timber Hill went through Ophir.

the Indian war whoop and saw the Redskins shoot his four companions down and charge into the camp. He did the only sensible thing left for him to do. He ran for cover and in doing so he ran out of the story for almost forty years.

What happened to the camp outfit, the livestock, or to the gold, Naked Face never knew, other than the evident fact that the Utes had taken possession of the stuff. He was so concerned in making his escape that he never had an opportunity to look back. What became of the gold, the camp outfit, and the pack stock was told many years later by several of the old Utes themselves—old warriors who participated in the massacre and had a part in the disposal of the stuff. Theirs was "first-hand" information. There were several of these old boys who gave their accounts of the massacre on different occasions and to different men; and those accounts all agree with each other remarkably well. Among these old Utes were Old Washington, Tallian, Gergorio, Pelon, and Narizon, all of them survivors of the white man's conquest of their homeland—and all of them bitter haters of the Whites. Page Wright, mentioned earlier, while not an actual participant in the raid, vividly remembered a great deal about it from his experiences, and from the stories he heard in his early childhood and youth; and he knew where that gold was buried, but like the other old Indians, he would never tell.

The Utes were so resentful of the white men after the latter took over the San Juan country, about twenty years subsequent to the massacre on the banks of the Piedra, that they would not associate with the Americans any more than circumstances compelled them, and they certainly confided no secret to the whites.

The Indians, however, did become friendly with the Mexicans of the region. The latter had taken homesteads along the creeks in the outlying areas where they had built modest homes, and used the ranches as headquarters for their livestock operations —raising sheep, goats, and some cattle. They and the Utes became friendly. By the early 1880's the Indians had told their story of the white men and the buried gold to enough of the early Mexican settlers of the region, like Juan Lucero, who lived down on the Pine river, Onesimo Archuleta, on the Piedra, and

Pedro Martinez on Cat creek above Pagosa Junction, that the yarn was widely known among the Spanish people and had become an inseparable part of the folklore of the region.

In fact it had become so generally known among the early-day Mexican residents that they had confused this yarn with the legend about a party of Frenchmen who had been in the San Juan basin hunting gold the previous century and had given the name of "La Francees" to Stolsteimer Creek, and even to this day the region about the mouth of that creek is still known as La Francees among the Mexicans of the area.

But the old Utes steadfastly refused to show their Mexican friends exactly where the gold was buried, or to give any bit of information that would be of any help in determining the precise spot. To do so, they staunchly maintained, would cause a violent death to the Indian that gave such information, to anyone other than a fellow Ute. And no Ute would ever uncover that gold. No curse, however, attached to revealing the general area in which the treasure was buried, or in recounting the history of the event.

Even though the story of the buried gold at the mouth of the Stolsteimer was quite widely known and was given absolute credence among the Mexican population, few white settlers knew anything about it, and those few took no interest in it. The white people had nothing in common with the Utes but hatred, and almost no social or economic contact with the Mexicans, so the story did not get about among them very much.

This ignorance, this unfortunate circumstance may have spoiled one wonderful opportunity that some white men later had of finding the lost treasure. Sometimes ignorance is a costly thing!

It was not until after the turn of the twentieth century that the old Utes began to get over their bitter hatred of the white men enough to become friendly with them and to tell them some past history of their tribe. The massacre and the hiding of the gold on the banks of the Piedra were fifty years in the past by that time, and many of the old Utes who had participated in those occurrences had by this time gone to their Happy Hunting Ground.

Among the few that were still alive to give a first-hand account of the event was Old Washington. With signs and a mixture of Spanish and Ute expressions, he told the story vividly, unhesitatingly, sincerely, and with remarkable clarity.

"Una vez, muncho ano pasado (one time, many years ago)," he always began his narrative, and would usually repeat,

"Una vez, muncho ano pasado, muncho ano," repeating the "muncho ano" as a sort of emphasis on the length of time, "five white men with horses and mules came from mas alla," indicating with a nod of his head and a pursing of his lips, a westerly direction. "These were shaggy-looking men like a buffalo with long black hair on their heads and faces, all, except one. This one had light hair on his head and no hair on his face, which made him appear so different from the others.

"We (the Utes) were camped back in the hills over there," pointing with his hand to the Ignacio Mountains.

"It was in the otoño (autumn) when the days were short, and the sun went to bed early. Most all of the Indians lived muy junto (close together) in one big camp in Vallecito De Los Pinos (the valley on upper Fosset creek) but some families had their own camp in other little parks away from our main camp. There were lots of acorns, lots of piñon nuts, and lots of fat game that year, and we were busy hunting and getting our food supply for the winter.

"These five white men suddenly rode up to one of these outlying camps. Only the women and children were in the camp at the time. The men were all out hunting. When the squaws and the papooses saw those fierce-appearing white men they were terribly scared, and ran away into the brush to hide. (Page Wright y suyo mamma (and his mother) lived in that camp.) Page was muy pequeno (very small) then. Those white men did a very bad thing, they stopped there long enough to take some food, and then they set that Indian camp on fire, and it all burned up. Foolish white men, to do an evil thing like that to a camp where there were only women and children—no Indian men to fight back. Why would they be so bad?

"Had those men only taken some food, the Indians would not have minded and we would not have bothered them, because we had plenty of food at that time, but when they set the camp on fire, that made all the Indians mad. One of those squaws came to the main camp and reported what had happened.

"It was almost dark by the time the Indian men got together and went to the place of the burned tepees. We found the horse tracks of the white men and followed them far enough to be sure they had gone down the canyon to the big river (Piedra) to make camp, but it was too dark for us to do anything more then.

"We built a big fire and had a war dance that night, and had a war council and planned to follow the men early the next morning, make a surprise attack on them, and kill them but not to kill or cripple their horses and mules if we could help it. We wanted that livestock, and the saddles, and whatever else of their camp outfit we could use.

"Cuando salto Lucero (When the morning star came up) we started after those white men. We located their camp easy enough, and crept along behind a bank until we were right up close to them, como aqui alla, (about from here to there)," indicating by gesture of his hand a large rock about a hundred feet away. "Foolish white men," and Old Washington chuckled with glee. "They were not on guard, and did not know we were there. They were awake but their heads were asleep. It was just before sunup. Four of the men were at the camp, all of them had lots of black whiskers all over their faces, but the other man was about 200 yards away," (again indicating the distance by pointing to a big pine tree); "He was driving the horses up to the camp. It seemed so strange that this man had no whiskers. He was naked faced!

"We did not want to injure any of the horses in the fight, so we decided to attack the men in the camp before the livestock came any nearer. We charged toward them from the bank, yelling and shooting as we went. Those white men didn't have a chance to grab their guns and fire a single shot at us. We killed them before they had time to do anything.

"The naked faced man got away. I was watching him, and when he saw us attack his companeros, he turned and ran away, and he ran so fast, lomismo que un caballo lijero (just like a race horse). He ran behind some brush and we did not see him any more. We did not try to follow him because the horses and mules had become excited with all the shooting and were running away, too, and we wanted them more than we did the naked faced man. So we let him go and rounded up the horses.

"We didn't find anything in the white men's camp that might have been stolen from the Indian camp the day before except some food—meat and bread—so the white men had not burned the camp to cover up some thievery, but had done it just to be mean. The white people could be so mean!

"We took all the white men's stuff except some gold they had. There were ten sacks of that stuff. Why were they so crazy about gold? The sacks were not very big but they were heavy. We didn't want the stuff, so we carried it over to a little ravine about a hundred feet away" (again indicating distance by a gesture to a clump of oak brush) "and dropped it, con ti saco (in its sacks) in that sanja (ditch or gutter). It was just a short, muy angosto (very narrow) little gully that the rain water had cut in a bank. It was so narrow that those sacks of gold fit into the bottom of it very tightly. No muy hondo arroyo (it was not very deep either) como asi (about like this)," holding his hands a couple of feet above the ground.

"We left the gold there, and the storm waters washed dirt over the gold and covered it all up. And it is still there to this day. I know because I go by there to see quite often. Many men have hunted for that spot but none of them have ever found it. No han escarvado en, el propio lujar (they have not dug in the right place)."

The most adroit of quizzing could never elicit more specific information about the location of the "propio lujar" from that astute old Indian. His reply was always the same, "alla donde se junta El Francees con La Piedra, poco serca" (over there where the Stolsteimer runs into the Piedra, nearby), and that general designation could cover a sizeable section of Archuleta county.

Old Washington died, peacefully as he sat asleep at the base of a big pine tree on his allotment along the Stolsteimer about the time of the First World War. His age at the time of his death was estimated to be 110 years. His life had been a long span, a link in the chain, connecting the unrecorded historic past of the

San Juan country with the turbulent present. And with his passing went one of the last human beings who had accurate, personal knowledge of the secret hiding place of a fabulous golden treasure.

But there was a time when there was one white man in the San Juan country that could have found that spot, and could have taken the gold out of it, if—. While that is not a big "if," it is an important one.

About the year 1890 a man drifted into the San Juan country and spent a part of the summer visiting a family by the name of Cooper. Coopers had a farm and were running a few cattle somewhere in the Pine river valley near the present town of Bayfield. Their visitor was Slim Carven or Cowen; the exact pronunciation of his last name is a little uncertain because of differences in the memories of old settlers in the region who knew the fellow. Carven seems to be the most generally accepted one. The man himself was not a man of mystery and made no secret of what his name was, but he did not mingle a great deal with the local folk.

Carven was about sixty or sixty-five years of age although he didn't appear to be more than forty. He was slender, of medium height, boyish in appearance, active, and agile. His face was as smooth as that of a school boy.

He helped the Coopers on the farm and on occasions he rode after their cattle. He was not hunting for anything while staying with the Coopers; he was just visiting them.

One afternoon, some two or three weeks after Slim Carven had arrived at the ranch and had had time to become familiar with the country, he startled Sam Cooper and a couple of other men visiting at the Cooper ranch with the remark: "I made a trip through this country nigh onto forty years ago."

"Why, man, there weren't any people livin' in this country at that time."

"There weren't no white folks, but there wuz lots of Indians."

His listeners wanted to hear more, so Carven related to them how he and his four partners had left California, bound for Santa Fe and the main trail east, with a string of seven mules, five of which were loaded with gold, how they forded the Colorado

194

river at Moab, and then proceeded into the San Juan country; how they had crossed the Pine river not far from the Cooper farm, and had headed into the Ignacio mountains. So far his account of their trip across the San Juan country agreed with that given by the Utes, as narrated by Washington and other old Indians of the tribe. The stories agreed up to the time that the white men encountered the isolated Indian camp in the little valley—and even after that point the stories still agreed as to the events that took place, but varied widely on interpretation of those events.

"How much gold didja say you had?" interposed one of his listeners.

"Five mule loads of the stuff, 'tween 650 and 700 pounds."

"Where didja get so much gold all at one time, and how didja get it, huh?"

"Don't yu' know it hain't polite to ask a feller where or how he got somethin'?" Carven parried a direct answer to the question. "We got the gold, never mind how, and we headed down through this here country, so as to avoid havin' inquisitive company along the way. We wuz sorta unsocial at that particular time."

"And how long ago didja say it was?" another listener wanted to know again.

"Nigh onto forty years."

"That don't seem possible. You don't look to be a day over forty right now. It don't look like you've ever even shaved yit."

"I haven't. I've never shaved in my life. I am a sort of freak. I don't grow whiskers. I am a sort of naked face."

Naked Face!

Slim Carven was one of those rare individuals, perhaps one in 50,000,000, who grow hair on the head, but no whiskers on the face. He never needed to shave.

"Well, get back to your story, naked face," jokingly remarked Cooper. "We want to hear the rest of the yarn."

"Hain't there some tall, sharp rocks, settin' on top of a long, high ridge over the other side of the divide yonder?" and Carven indicated the divide between the Pine and the Piedra watersheds later named Ignacio Mountains. "Hain't no other rocks like 'em in the whole country."

"Yes. Them's the Chimney Rocks, over on the divide between Stolsteimer and the Piedra."

"Then I am right and this is the place. We crossed the Pine down below here and follered up a little canyon to the top of the divide over yonder. Jest over the top of the ridge we ran onto an Indian camp. It was jest a small camp—only three or four tepees bunched together in a little park up there. We ran onto that camp kinda sudden like. We were jest as surprised as the Indians were. There weren't no bucks at the camp, just squaws and kids. When the squaws saw us they let out a devil of a squawl, and them and the kids took to the oak brush on the run.

"They didn't need to run. We wasn't going to do them no harm. Trouble was the last thing in the world we wanted just then. We wuz goin' to ride right on by the camp and not pay no 'tention to it. But the squaws had left some meat cookin' by the fire when they ran away, and the Indians had a lot of other meat a hangin' around there. Us fellows had been a runnin' on short rations fer several days—we hadn't seen no game to kill, and we wuz purty hungry—and gosh, that meat shore smelled good. We decided to take some of it along with us. There was nobody there to object, and the Indians had plenty. We didn't figger that they 'ud mind sharin' up a little bit. Specially when nobody wuz there to say no. Me and one of the other fellers stopped to gather up the grub while the rest of the bunch went on with the mules. We got some of the meat, not very much, and some bread, and it didn't take us long to do it, but in the meantime the other boys wuz going out 'o sight around a turn in the valley, and we wuz gettin' a bit nervous. Too nervous, I guess, 'cause when I went to get on my horse, with a bunch of that grub in one hand, he shied away from me and I had a little trouble in mountin' him. In the ruckus we knocked one of those tepees over—jest knocked it over was all, we didn't mess up the camp any. 'Twouldn't amount to nuthin' to set that tepee back up again, but we didn't take time for that. We figgered the Indians could do that, and that they would pay no attention to such a little chore. It wuz while we wuz goin' down the draw after we

196

got the meat from the Indian camp that I saw those sharp rocks on that high ridge, and I saw 'em again several times the next day as I was gettin' out of the country, and I ain't ever forgot 'em.

"We went on down to the main river (the Piedra) to camp that night. It was gettin' kinda dark by the time we got there, and we scouted around a bit to find a suitable campground. It was a beautiful valley there, and lots of grass—jest like a meadow. I remember we camped on an open bench where there was a sort of bank jest back of our camp, and oakbrush skirting part way around the flat, to make it easier to watch our horses during the night. We had a good supper on Indian venison. And that came mighty near bein' my last supper on earth. It wuz the last supper fer my four pardners.

"The Redskins, damn 'em, attacked us by surprise, jest afore sunup next morning. They killed the four other boys right in the camp, and the only reason they didn't get me too wuz that I wuz about 200 yards away driving the horses and mules up to the camp.

"I heered the shots and the war whoops when the Indians attacked and I saw my pardners fall. It didn't take me no time to realize what had happened. The sudden racket stampeded the horses. They whirled and started to run away, and I run, too, run for the oakbrush on the edge of the flat. I never ran faster in my life. I had about forty yards to go and it didn't take me long to make it. I expected to get shot on the way, or to hear the blood-urdlin' yell of these cussed Indians chasin' me, but nuthin' happened. Mebbe they didn't see me. Anyhow, I got away. And I kept agoin'. I couldn't do my pardners no good— they wuz already dead, and I didn't have no gun with me except my pistol, and only a little ammunition fer it. The Indians were still makin' a lot of racket back at our camp. I cud hear 'em, but I cudn't see 'em from where I wuz, and I didn't take time to try, I wuz runnin' through the brush as fast as I cud when I stumbled over a sharp rock stickin' up about a foot out of the ground. I remember that rock mighty well, 'cause I skinned my shin purty bad when I stumbled on it, and my pistol flew out of its scabbard and landed on the open ground at the edge of the

patch of brush. That sore shin bothered me for several days. I
was afraid the Indians would see me when I picked my pistol up,
but I guess they didn't. None of 'em ever caught up with me
anyway.

"I don't know whatever happened to our camp, to the horses
and mules or to the gold. I didn't stay to see. I was left afoot
and cud do nuthin' with any of it anyhow. Of course the Indians
would take the horses and the saddles. They cud use them, and
they'd take the camp outfit too, or would burn it up. They
wouldn't want the gold. They had no use for that. But they'd
carry it off and throw it away somewhere, and the Lord only
knows where. I made my getaway while I cud.

"And I hain't ever been back to that place since. I am going to
ride over there some day, afore I leave here, and look around.
I had some purty tough goin' gettin' out of this country then, but
I finally made it out to a Mexican settlement called Abuquiu over
on the Rio Grande. Later on I went on down to Santa Fe, but
I never told nobody about what had happened, and I didn't
make no fuss about it either. I didn't want nobody to know
about that gold. I had already had trouble enough, and there
wuz men in authority back in Californy at that time that would
have been mighty glad to hear something about that bullion, and
would have made it purty hot fer me. So I kept my mouth shet.

"But you wouldn't think them Indians would'uve gotten so
mad about a little grub and an upset tepee, now, would you?"

Cooper and the other men who had heard Carven's story allowed "as how the Indians behaved purty strange" sometimes,
but that their actions on this occasion were quite extraordinary.
Had the white men known, at that time, the Indian version of the
story, they would not have thought the savages had acted so
strange. But none of the white people had yet ever heard the
Indian side of the yarn, although it was, even then, common
knowledge among the Mexican folk of the region.

No one doubted the truthfulness of Carven's story or ques-
tioned his veracity; nor did anyone think his actions strange
under the circumstances. These men were all pioneers themselves
and could readily accept such extraordinary conditions and

events as Carven had related. Indeed, many strange things happened on the American frontier.

Carven rode over onto the Piedra a few days after he had told the men his story. He wanted Cooper to go with him, but the rancher could not get away at the time, and Carven went alone.

When Carven returned that evening he told Cooper: "I found the place all right, and I saw those Chimney Rocks agin, and there hain't no mistake about them being the same rocks I saw forty years ago. We camped down at the point of the ridge them rocks is on. Of course there wuz nuthin' right on the spot to show jest where our camp wuz, no ashes, no bones, no gold, no nuthin' but I know I found it 'cause I found the rock I skinned my shin on. It was still stickin' up out of the ground in that clump of brush, and I know our camp was on the upper end of that little flat that that brush wuz on, not more'n three hundred yards from that rock. I'm namin' that rock The Monument to my Lost Fortune, cause it was there that I lost my gold."

Of course Carven did not know it, but he was within 100 feet, possibly nearer than that, maybe he even walked over the top of his lost fortune, while he was scouting around his old campsite that day. Old Washington said the Indians dumped it into a shallow ravine not more than 100 feet from the camp—but Carven didn't know that. Sometimes ignorance can be an expensive thing.

After a few more days spent with the Coopers, Carven moved on to other parts. Like other men who had lived on the frontier many years, he was a restless soul and was always hunting for the "greener grass just over the mountain." No one ever heard of him again, although a few years later, Cooper and other white men who knew about Carven's story tried mighty hard to find him.

It was ten or twelve years after Carven had visited the Coopers and had told his story before the white people had become friendly enough with the Mexicans to swap stories with them and had heard from them the Indian version of the yarn.

The Indian story and Carven's account dovetailed together too perfectly to be just coincidence; and the fact that, according to the Indians, there was one man in the group who had no whiskers, who was a "naked face" and the only one who had gotten way alive, made the deciding clincher that the two stories were concerning the same event. The two separate accounts complemented each other. It took both of them together to make the full story complete; and the two of them, when put together, told where to find that fabulous fortune in gold bullion.

The Indians had thrown the gold into a ravine about 100 feet from the camp, and Carven had definitely located that old camp within a very small area, by finding the unmistakable landmark, the rock over which he had stumbled, years before when he was making his escape.

But where was Carven?

And so the buried gold is still buried somewhere on the Piedra near the mouth of the Stolsteimer waiting for some lucky discoverer to come along and find it. And that discovery can happen almost any time. Natural floodwaters cut that little ravine there in the first place, and then washed the dirt over those sacks of bullion, so the water can, when natural conditions are right again, wash that covering earth off, and leave exposed that generous golden fortune for anyone who passes by and has eyes sharp enough to see it.

If you are ever out Piedra way near the mouth of the Stolsteimer be sure to take a careful look into all the little ravines you cross. It could be a $400,000 look.

SEQUEL

Temple H. Cornelius commented in "Letters to the Editor" of the Durango *News* about Page Wright, 104-year-old Indian of Southern Ute Tribe, and a story about him in the *News* issue of October 9, 1955:

"Page Wright was a real old timer in the San Juan. He was the only living person who knew from actual first hand information the exact location of the famous Stewart Placer and the spot where the Utes dumped five mule loads of bullion on the Piedra River somewhere below Chimney Rock.

"The Utes killed four white men on their way from California with ten bags of gold bars. The Utes took the horses and mules and such other stuff as they wanted of the white men and hid the gold for which they had no use.

"In 1896 Dick Keller was the assayer at Durango Smelter when an old Ute Indian and his squaw came to the office with a bright metal bar about one inch square and six inches long. He pointed to the bar and demanded that 'You makeum money.'

The assayers were busy and ordered the Indians away.

"This could have been some of the gold from Chimney Rock area."

Talk and Share It

The Gallegos family lived on their isolated little farm on the south bank of the San Juan River opposite the depot and water tank of the Denver & Rio Grand Western Railroad at Arboles, Colorado.

This had been the Gallegos home since about 1890 when Manuel Gallegos, Sr., had taken up the land as a homestead and had brought his family there to live. Here the Gallegos children —three girls and two boys—had been raised.

No other homes were in the immediate vicinity. There wasn't room. The high, rocky tablelands on each side of the river came so close together here that there was no valley along the stream bed in this area. On the north side there was only room enough for the railway between the river and the base of the hills. On the south side a narrow strip of land, containing ten or fifteen acres, lay along the bank of the river between the stream bed and a higher bench covered with scattered sage and boulders, that sloped back a short distance to the foot of the high tableland to the south. The Gallegos house was on the edge of this bench. From this vantage point the Gallegos family could watch the daily arrival and departure of the D. & R. G. W. passenger trains from the station across the river. If a passenger or two disembarked from the train at the station, that was an event to be noted with interest by the family—particularly by young Manuelito, a slight, friendly youth in his late teens. Manuelito loved to talk in English or Spanish. He had attended the country school near Arboles until he had attained the ripe, legal age of 16 after which time the law no longer required him to "gastar" (waste) his time in the schoolroom. By that time he could speak the King's English fairly well, if allowances were made for his outrageous disregard of the rules of syntax and grammar.

The only trail leading up to the top of this high mesa passed by the Gallegos home and wound its way up through the timber and broken rimrock for five miles to the top of the rugged hillside. That trail was there when Gallegos, Sr., moved onto his homestead. Legend had it that this was an old Indian trail that had existed since "the memory of man runneth not to the contrary," and was used by early white men, bandits, and robbers in the region.

In fact the legend included a rich cache of gold coins and gold bullion buried near the mouth of a shallow cave under the sandstone rimrock near the point where this trail come out onto the high mesa. This legend was common knowledge among the Mexican settlers of that region.

According to this story many years previously, even before the U. S. Army had subdued the Ute Indians in the area, and when robbery and thievery were in flower there, two older men had a crude rock shanty near the portal of this cave. Using this remote hideout as a headquarters, these old fellows sallied forth periodically to rob stagecoaches and travelers to and from California. They brought the booty from these raids back to this place to hide until such time as they wanted to take it away. Before they could do this, however, a small band of Utes attacked them, killed one, and stole their horses. The other man was wounded in the fight but managed to escape and made his way to Abiquiu, the nearest Mexican settlement more than 100 miles away on the Rio Grande River. A Mexican family there took him into their home and cared for him until he died from his wounds a few weeks later.

In the accepted form for legends in such conditions, the bandit out of gratitude for this kindness told the family about the cache and gave them a map and description of its location and instructions how to find it. In other words a "derrotero," a sort of way-bill to the treasure.

This legend became common knowledge among the Mexican settlers of the San Juan region. Gallegos, Sr., knew about it. He did not know the exact location of the cache, but from descriptions he had heard around many an evening campfire he was sure the treasure was buried on a little bench near the mouth of a shallow cave under the upper sandstone rim a short way east from the point where the trail came out on the high mesa south of his homestead. He found the ruins of an old stone cabin, an old stone fireplace, and a short trail of sorts from the top of the mesa down onto this narrow bench, and a spring (or at least a seep) that apparently had been hollowed out by hand years before in the back of the cave. He made several exploratory trips to the place in search of the cache, but he never made any excavations at likely spots to see what might be underground. He confined his explorations to looking and speculating, but not to spading—that required work. He always postponed that part until mañana.

Sometime before he died Gallegos, Sr., took his two sons up to "el entierro de nosotros" (the buried treasure of ours) and told them the story about the cache. At that time Fermin, the oldest son, was eighteen years old, and Manuelito was ten. In conformity to the rule of primogeniture adhered to by the Mexican people, Fermin would become head of the family on the death of his father. It would be his responsibility to look after the family and the family would be accountable to him.

After his father died, Fermin followed in his footsteps. He worked for wages to supplement the family income. He herded sheep for stockmen in the region during the winter, and helped other farmers in the area a few days at a time in hay harvest during the summer. Between times he was home with nothing to do. Manuelito stayed home all the time to irrigate the crop, cultivate the beans and chili—and visit with any chance passerby.

Many times the brothers talked about the cache and how rich they would be when they would dig it up. But always the digging was to be mañana. It would be a major project, they figured, that would require time and money to do and machinery to do it with. In fact to them it grew to be such an important undertaking that the use of such simple tools as a pick and shovel in hunting for it would be alomst sacrilege. But always mañana they would have the wherewithal to do the work properly and successfully. In the meantime, they could keep dreaming.

Came a day late in August about 1912 when a couple of Anglo strangers got off the westbound passenger train at Arboles. All the baggage they had were a couple of knapsacks. They got directions from the station agent at Arboles how to get to the

Gallegos ranch and immediately set out to cross the river to the place. Manuelito, who had been watching from the house, met them as they walked off the rustic footbridge. Fermin was at Bayfield at the time helping in the hay and grain harvest there.

"Hello," was his cheerful greeting. "You ben lookit for me?"

Each of the strangers gave the other a sly look as one of them replied: "We sure have. You are just the fellow we want to see."

The remark pleased Manuelito. It made him feel important to be told that someone had come purposely to see him.

"Whata for you wanta see me?"

"We have heard that you know about a buried treasure in this vicinity and we would like for you to tell us about it."

"Sure I know about un entierro. He belongit to me and my brudder. But he be it a long way from here upa that hillside to the top." And with a nod of his head he indicated the ledged-ribbed side of the mountain to the south.

"How far?"

"Mebbe five miles, mebbe so, more far."

"Is the place hard to find?"

"He be too hard to find. No estranjero (stranger) could finda that lugar (place)."

"Are you sure you can find it again?"

"Sure I be sure. I cana go there even in la escurana (darkness)."

"You're sure a smart boy to know such a rough country so well, and to know where a cache is. Don't many people know things like that. We'd like to see the place if you can find it again. We'll give you $5 to show it to us."

Manuelito was pleased by the flattery and by the opportunity to earn a "five spot" for himself. He readily agreed to take the strangers to the place. The men helped him catch and saddle the ponies. These were general utility animals; like the old Model T Ford, they were used for whatever job that required motive power—from pulling a plow to being ridden to a Sunday-go-to-meeting party anywhere in the area. However, only two saddles were available, both of ancient vintage and of years of rough use and neglect. Manuelito graciously let his guests have the saddles and he rode bareback.

"Whata for you takeit la mochila?" he asked as the men picked up their knapsacks to take along.

"Oh, we might need 'em," said one of the fellows as he adroitly poked the protruding end of a short shovel handle back down out of sight. His companion however was not so successful in keeping his bit of equipment concealed. When he swung his knapsack onto the saddle horn, the sharp point of a prospector's pick jutted through the canvass and jabbed his horse in the shoulder. The pony promptly bucked the whole thing off. In order to readjust his pack, he had to dig the pick out of his knapsack.

"What that herramienta (tool) be for?" Manuelito asked.

"That's to help us find our directions so we won't get lost," the man explained. "We set the hammer end of it on the ground, sight toward the sun over the sharp point, and that way know what direction we want to go."

Manuelito accepted this nonsensical explanation without further comment since that was a tool he had never seen.

The trail up the mountain wound and twisted around huge slabs of sandstone, followed along narrow benches between sandstone ledges, and wormed its way up through notches in the rimrock. The traveling was slow but made all the more opportunity for conversation.

Because of adroit questioning on the part of the strangers, and an enthusiastic willingness to talk by Manuelito, before they had arrived at the top of the mesa, the men had pumped him for all the information and exaggerations he had about the cache.

Why hadn't he dug up the buried treasure before this time?

Well, to dig up that tesoro (treasure) was a major project. It would require a lot of work, equipment, time, and expense. Neither he nor his brother had had time or money to do the job. But some day (mañana) they would, and once that task was done they would be rich men—much rico.

To clinch his argument, he sagely repeated an old Mexican adage of the mining region: "It takes one rich mine (income from) to develop another rich mine." No explanation of how the first rich mine was to be developed.

A short distance after "topping out" on the high tableland,

Manuelito turned sharply to the left along the crest of the mesa and soon conducted los Americanos down a short trail through the scrub timber onto a narrow bench below the primary sandstone rim.

"Here be el lugar (the spot)," he said.

The place was similar to countless other in this sedimentary formation. A narrow bench in a sort of horseshoe shape, with the heel of the shoe spread abnormally wide, and a shallow cave (known locally as an "eyebrow") under the primary sandstone bluff at the toe of the shoe. At the back of this cave was a spring (more properly known locally as a seep). Clumps of scrub oak, buck brush, willow, and other moisture-loving perennial plants, indigenous to the region, grew in scattered groups along the bench at the base of the overhanging bluff and partially concealing the mouth of the cave. At the far end of the bench was the tumbled remains of a rock wall that had at some past time enclosed a niche in the bluff. The cabin had been so constructed that this niche made a crude, natural fireplace in one corner and smoke stains on the side of the cliff immediately above the spot gave further proof of this condition. The door of the cabin faced south, which gave the occupants of the shack an unobstructed view of the trail descending onto the other end of the bench. There were no other indications of previous occupancy of the spot. No artificial markings anywhere to indicate a location of buried treasure or anything else. High up on the sheer sandstone bluff at the south end of the bench and in plain sight from the cabin door was a natural landmark. It was a round hole, perhaps six inches in diameter and stained a deep, dark brown on the inside and with streaks of brown coloration extending from it down the face of the cliff. Holes like this one occurred frequently in the sedimentary formations of the region. They were made by erosion. In past ages when the sandstone was laid down, small masses of softer material rich in iron oxide accumulated in these spots, and exposure to wind, rain, and surface water washed this material out but left the harder rock around it intact.

The strangers took special note of this lone landmark.

"Where do you figure the treasure is buried?" they asked Manuelito.

"I be dammit if I know," he said. "No alli marcas negunas (there are no marks) to show it where. We haffa to dig it up the whole place to finda that tesoro."

"That sure would be a big job. You were right when you said it would take a lot of work and money to do this."

"Sure I be right. I been figure this proposicion for long time. For dis reason I no do before."

And he made this remark with evident pride that his conclusions had been confirmed by these Americanos. He was highly flattered by the outcome.

"Tell you what we will do. We think there is a big fortune buried here. Enough to make all of us rich. You take the horses and go back down to the ranch, and we will cut across country to Chama to save time; and in a few days we will come back to Arboles with enough supplies and tools to do this job. You be ready to pack the stuff up here and help supervise the work. We will need your 'headwork' very much to get this job done. In fact we won't be able to do it without your help."

Manuelito was elated by these remarks. That he was indispensable to the success of the project was highly gratifying to him. The apparent eagerness of the men to get the supplies immediately and get the work underway without delay was similarly very impressive to him.

It never occurred to him that Chama was more than forty miles northeast across rough country; that the journey there on foot would require at least two days; that the men could return to Arboles with him, catch the morning train, and be in Chama by noon the next day.

He readily assented to their proposition. The men took their knapsacks and trudged up the short trail ahead of Manuelito and the horses. At the edge of the mesa they turned easterly in the general direction of Chama, and Manuelito, pleased with the outcome of the day's work, took the trail down the mountain to home, dreaming all the while about how he would spend his riches.

The following day Manuelito was at the station when the train arrived to welcome his companeros. By what miracle he expected the men to perform such a feat is unfathomable. He was disappointed that they did not come. It was even more disappointing when they didn't arrive the second day. But he was still filled with enthusiasm when his brother Fermin came home from the hay harvest that evening. He gave Fermin a glowing account of what had happened and finished with the conclusion that now, at long last, they were going to be rich from their tesoro just as soon as the two Americanos came back with the necessary supplies to do the excavating. Fermin, however, failed to share in this enthusiasm. He knew the tricky ways of some Americanos. He "threw a lot of cold water" on Manuelito's enthusiasm with the remark:

"Perdas sus espanranzes (give up your hopes). Those ladrones (thieves) have tricked you. No van a volver (they will not return). They have already gotten el tesoro and are gone. Mañana we shall see."

Early the next morning the two brothers made the trip up to the cave.

They found a freshly excavated pit a couple of feet wide and about three feet long, dug in the soft earth at the base of the bluff, and directly below the round brown-stained hole in the sandstone above. In the moist sand at the bottom of the pit were two separate and distinct impressions of containers of some sort. On the ground adjacent to the pit were the rotted remains of two rawhide pack bags, and by the side of these lay the prospector's pick and the short shovel that Manuelito had seen in the Americanos' knapsacks. But the Americanos were nowhere around; neither was the treasure.

Martin Hotter's Famous Rock

The most famous rock ever found in the San Juan country of southwestern Colorado was the one discovered by the late Martin Hotter in the summer of 1897, on the bank of Junction creek, just below the mouth of Walls Gulch, in the La Plata mountains about fifteen miles northwest of Durango. It was a big rock and contained a small fortune in rich gold ore.

Countless numbers of men have eagerly searched the adjacent mountain slopes on each side of the Junction Creek canyon since then in an intense effort to find the place from which that huge stone came. For at that spot, they believe, exists the largest and richest sylvanite ore vein in all the La Platas, one which could pay a king's ransom and still leave a tremendous golden fortune for its discoverers.

Martin Hotter was not an experienced mining man, and he discovered the rich content of this rock quite by accident. Scores of other men had seen this stone before Hotter did. It lay out in plain sight of anyone who passed by that way and was only a few feet from the main trail up Junction Creek. Hundreds of prospectors and miners had traveled over that trail before, without noticing it. Hotter paused at that spot one day late in the summer of 1897, to eat his lunch, and he used the huge stone as his seat while he did so. It was then that he noticed a streak or band about eight to ten inches wide, of a different material, traversing the entire thickness of the rock.

Hotter, a native of Austrian Tyrol, had been working for Ben Shears and Ed Biggs, lessors of the Bessie G Mine, for several months previous to this time. On this occasion he had taken a few days leave from his job and was on his way to Durango for a short rest and celebration.

The Bessie G mine is located high up in the La Platas, a considerable distance beyond the mouth of Walls Gulch. The trail between the mine and Durango was the one that lay in the bottom of the Junction Creek canyon. It was a full day's hike either way between the mine and town, so a man making it needed to take a lunch. Hotter had a lunch with him and selected this big rock as the place to eat it.

It was a large stone, "as big as a cook stove," Hotter said in describing it, "and while eating my lunch there I noticed its peculiar formation. It was like a giant sandwich with a thick streak of the dark ore thru the middle of it."

Hotter was not sure that the darker material in the rock was really ore, but he knew it was very similar to the rich sylvanite that was being mined at the Bessie G; so when he returned from his vacation in Durango a few days later, he broke off a piece of that darker material and took it to the mine with him to show to the men there. They were both experienced miners and would be able to identify the rock.

"When I showed them the specimen," said Hotter, "their eyes bugged out and they became intensely interested in it. I thought for a minute I had really found something. The men looked at each other, and sort of winked, and nodded their heads very slightly to each other. They did not say whether the ore had any value or not, but merely asked me if I could find the big rock again, and how big it was, and a dozen other questions about it. But I did not suspicion anything wrong. I thought they were figuring me as a greenhorn and were trying me out to see if I could go back to that big rock."

Hotter arrived at the mine, showed the specimen, and told Shears and Biggs about his find, late one evening. He was surprised the following morning when his employers announced their intentions of going to town themselves that day. They had made no previous mention of any such plans. But Shears remarked to Hotter:

"Martin, you have had your layoff, and now it is our turn to go celebrate. We are going down this morning, and you can come along with us, and see if you can find that big rock again, and show it to us, then you can come back up here and watch the mine while we are gone. You do not have to do any work while we are away. Just stay and watch after the outfit so no one will steal anything from us."

211

"I thought that was pretty easy for me," said Hotter, "not to have to work and yet get paid for my time, so I went along and showed them that I could find that rock again. They looked the big rock over very carefully when we got to it, and admitted that it was a very peculiar formation, but said that peculiar formations were very common in these mountains. Apparently that was the end of the affair because they prepared to go on to town, so I left them and returned to the mine. It took them a long time to celebrate, because they did not return to the mine for 10 days."

Shears and Biggs were not celebrating, however, in the way Hotter thought they were. They recognized the ore in that rock as rich sylvanite and knew there was enough of it to amount to a very substantial sum. They only traveled a little way down the trail after Martin left them. When they figured he was safely out of sight and hearing, they returned and broke up that huge stone. They sorted out the ore and sacked it and left the fragments of valueless country rock lying on the spot, and there those fragments remained until washed away in the flood of 1911. The writer saw them there numberless times from 1904 until the big flood.

Shears and Biggs took the ore to the Durango smelter and received almost $1600 cash in return for it. "But they never gave this damn Dutchman one penny of it," said Hotter later. "They spent all of that money and more too trying to find where that came from but never found out." Nor has any one else ever found the place from which that rich stone came, altho a countless number of men have diligently searched for it—and still do—in the years that have intervened since Martin Hotter found the stone.

The rock was not just a loose bit of float easily carried from some distant point to the place of its discovery by the forces of nature. It was so heavy it had not traveled far from the ledge of which it was an original part, and that traveling had been down hill.

It is certain this piece of ore originated somewhere in that immediately vicinity and was carried by natural forces to the place where it was found. Human hands did not bring it there. The force of gravity, of course, was the major factor in the moving of this heavy stone, but flood and avalanche may have been assisting forces. It is only logical to conclude that somewhere higher up on those adjacent verdant mountain sides exists the virgin ledge whose extent and richness have never yet been explored. It is perhaps covered with soil, possibly only a few inches deep, but sufficient, nevertheless, to conceal any surface out-cropping that might betray its location. Some day, natural forces will again remove that protecting coat, leaving the vein exposed to view once more, and fortunate, indeed, will be the individual who is lucky enough to be the one that passes that way again.

The Old Florida Mine

Some 30 miles back in the rough mountain country northeast of Durango, Colorado, lies a rich mineral district. Roughly, this territory embraces all the southerly slope of the Needle mountain between the Las Animas river canyon on the west and the Vallecito canyon on the east. It includes within its boundaries the entire watershed of the Florida river—the source of Durango's water supply. The old Florida mine is in this area and took its name from this stream. In this district also are located several other mines that were successfully and profitably worked by the pioneer miners of the white race. Some of this mining was done before the time that any established communities were made in the adjacent country. The city of Pueblo was then the nearest trading center, and it was approximately 300 miles away, but it was the nearest point where the ore from the Florida district could be sold.

Logically, only very rich ore could be profitably transported so far by pack animals. The early miner in this district was prospecting in virgin territory; he worked only those veins that were very rich and would pay from the very surface of the ground. And all the work he did on any vein after he found it was in pay dirt.

Due to the hostility of the Ute Indians, and the natural disadvantages connected with mining in this region, activities came to a standstill for a number of years following these early discoveries. In the late eighties and early nineties, however, mining was renewed on a far more extensive scale. It was during this later period that several big producing mines were successfully worked in this district. The most famous of these was the Old Pittsburgh, which was said to have produced more than a million dollars worth of ore before a dispute between the employees and the management closed it down. The many log cabins used as residences by the miners are still to be found near that old mine. They are in a very bad state of decay now, but their number gives some clue to the large crew of men employed at one time. This particular settlement is called Log Town and is one of the most interesting ghost towns of the San Juan basin.

The Florida area was a cherished hunting ground of the redskins. It was a beautiful country, abounding in game and fish, and the Indians took a great deal of pleasure in roaming over its verdant hills and valleys. For several years after the land had been ceded to the United States by the Ute Indians, small bands of these people would return each summer to spend a short time in these mountains.

On such trips to and from the mountains, some of these bands would purchase food at the Waldner ranch on the upper Florida. In payment for the food and hospitality given to them on these occasions, the Utes would give gold nuggets, frequently to the value of $500. The payments always far exceeded the value of the food and were always voluntarily given. This was a profitable transaction for the white man, but he did not want to "kill the goose that was laying the golden egg" by robbing the Indians and thereby driving their trade somewhere else; so he remonstrated on one occasion that the pay was excessive, and offered to return a part of it, to which proposition an Indian replied:

"Indian no eat gold. He like-um white man grub. White man like-um gold. Indian like trade. Why white man no like?"

And the Utes would take no refund. To the paleface's argument that they would soon exhaust their gold supply at such a rate of trading, the redskin replied: "Indian know where heap gold. If white man knew, white man could put gold shoe on his horses. Indian no tell."

And the Indians never did tell. Later attempts of the white men to follow them to this rich treasure came to naught.

This Indian gold came from the same area in the mountains where the Old Florida mine is located. It might have come from the mine itself. Let us turn our attention to the study of that fabulously rich diggings which has already made several men rich, and in whose darkened precincts there still remains sufficient gold and silver to enrich many more.

The existence and the history of the Florida mine might never

215

have been known in the San Juan basin but for the coming of a stranger to this country in the spring of 1928. He was about sixty-five years of age. Apparently he was a man of wealth, and he gave his name as Thurman. He stayed at the best hotel while in Durango, quietly went about his business, and always had plenty of money with which to pay any obligations he incurred. He made inquiries about the country but told no one his business.

After a few days' time he engaged two local men with pack horses to take him on a pack trip to the headwaters of the Florida river. Not until the second day out did he give these men any specific information as to his purpose or destination. Then he told them he was hunting for an old mine at the foot of Big Elk mountain, and requested to be taken to that vicinity. Upon being informed by his guides that they did not know of such a mountain on the Florida drainage, he instructed them to proceed to a mesa whose eastern rim was formed by a limestone formation. The guides knew where that was, and took him directly to the eastern side of Lime mesa, at which point they camped. They did very little work for the first few days there. Thurman studied the lay of the country. He explored the bottoms of all the adjacent canyons and ascended to the tops of the nearby hills, from which points of vantage he carefully studied the whole surrounding country.

One evening he returned to the camp, apparently satisfied with his decision. He remarked to his companions: "We are in the right section of the mountains, all right, but I do not yet know whether we are in the right locality or not. That remains to be ascertained. Tomorrow we begin work in earnest."

Briefly he told the men what to look for. The mine he sought consisted of a shaft sunk in the solid rock near the bed of a mountain stream, he told them. It was in the floor of some one of these narrow mountain valleys. Not far from this shaft was a cabin built in the timber, near the edge of a bluff. The cabin faced east, overlooking this bluff. It had a doorway and two windows in the easterly end, and there were four bunks, two lower and two upper, built out of poles, along the inside of the south wall. The shanty might be very dilapidated, he said, but if a substantial part of it was still standing, he could identify it. It had been built more than fifty years before this present expedition.

When several days' searching in the vicinity failed to reveal the location of either the shaft or the cabin, Thurman determined to check on his position in another way.

Accordingly, he told his men: "I was just a kid when I first came into this country with my father and my uncle. We did not come in here the way you fellows brought me this trip. We came up the Animas river canyon to a point west of here, where we had a blazed trail leading out of that canyon and across country to this watershed. The trail was not blazed all the way to the mine, however. Many of those blazed trees should still be there. Let us go and see if we can find them."

In conformity with this new plan, they moved their camp over onto the breaks of the Animas canyon and began to search for these old markings. It was not many days before they found the blazes, just as Thurman said they should, and were able to trace them from the bottom of the canyon up the rugged mountainside, over onto the Florida drainage, exactly as Thurman had previously described. The blazes were very old. Their age was self evident.

The writer discovered this old blazed trail a number of years ago, and followed the blazes for a sufficient distance at that time to prove to himself that they marked a definite trail in bygone years. The writer had not yet heard of the Old Florida mine when he found these markings.

This additional proof of the correctness of his location gave Thurman new stimulus in his search. The camp was returned to the vicinity of Lime mesa, where Thurman continued his quest with greater zeal. He was not successful, however, in finding either the shaft or the cabin in the remaining time he had at his disposal that summer. But he was not melancholy when he left. He paid the men what he owed them in cash and never complained in the least about the size of the bill. He promised to return the following year to renew the search. He never told anyone whether the mine was rich or not, nor did he try to promote it, or endeavor to interest anyone else in it in any way.

True to his promise, he came back during the summer of 1929

to pursue again the hunt begun the year before. He hired several local men, stockmen, and others familiar with this mountain district, to assist him in his search this time. He told them what he was hunting for and offered a substantial bonus to any of them who would find either the cabin or the shaft.

He made the acquaintance of other stockmen in the region and of them he made inquiries relative to the old cabin and the old mine. To Chester Petty, a local sheepman whose cool judgment and high integrity were above reproach, he told the following story:

"I am hunting for an old mine up here in this country, but, lest you think me crazy, I will tell you its history. More than fifty years ago my father found a rich vein here. Our family lived in Pueblo at the time. Father brought some of the ore home with him, and upon being assayed it proved to be very valuable.

"The following three summers my father, my uncle, my older brother, and myself came out here and mined on that lead. I was only a kid then. I did not do much work. I came along with them, nevertheless. During those three summers, we made five trips to Pueblo with our pack horses loaded with ore. That ore net us the magnificent sum of $125,000. This amount was a stupendous fortune in those days.

"The dangers, disadvantages, and hardships associated with mining under the conditions that obtained in this country at that time were very great. My folks decided to give up their mining activities after the third summer and go to South America to engage in cattle raising. They did that. The money they made in mining here, they invested in land and cattle there. Those investments formed the foundation of my fortune now, and it is a very substantial one. Judged by the standards of this country, I am a millionaire.

"I am not hunting for this mine because I need it. I am financially well enough fixed without it, but I dislike to think of so much wealth lying here idle, when it might just as well be active and doing somebody some good. You know, I thought I could go right to it, but I have not been able to yet.

"The mine consisted of a shaft about 80 feet deep, and a short tunnel on the lead at the bottom of the shaft. It was sunk in the solid rock in the bottom of a canyon, near a small stream of water. The cabin was in some timber on a rim not far away. My time will not now permit me to stay here very much longer. If I don't find it, it will pay you to keep a lookout for it. It will make you rich if you find it. The shaft, of course, may be filled with debris, and overgrown with vegetation, but I can find it, even so, if I find the cabin."

It was not many days after this conversation took place that Thurman received a message calling him away. He was in Durango with one of his men when he got the message. He did not return to the camp. Instead, he gave his companion the other men's wages in full to the following Saturday night, together with his address, and the request that they keep a sharp watch for the cabin, whenever they chanced to be in this locality in the future; and if any of them found it, to communicate with him.

Of course, his leaving brought an end to the expedition. Most of the men took no further interest in the matter. One of them, however, a local cowboy by the name of Charley Waldner, continued to search for the cabin whenever he could do so. Some two years later, he found a cabin which suited the description. It was in a clump of spruce trees on a rimrock in an inconspicuous place not so very far from Lime mesa. He was convinced he had found the right cabin, but Thurman's address had been carelessly misplaced in the meantime. No one else had his address, and to this date Waldner has found no way in which to communicate with him.

Waldner's discovery may be the key with which to unlock the whereabouts of that fortune, but he does not know how to apply it, and he cannot find the man who does know. Thurman left without telling how far or in what direction the shaft was from the cabin.

Incomplete knowledge can be a very provoking thing, sometimes.

The fact that Thurman did not find the shaft does not prove that it never existed. It was left exposed, and unprotected from the elements, and as he said, could easily have been filled up

The Cache of Gold on Falls Creek

In a shallow pit scooped out by hand in the soft leafmold under a clump of spruce trees on the headwaters of Falls Creek, in southwestern Colorado, is a rich little fortune of more than $60,000 in gold nuggets waiting for someone to come and get it. I knew the man who put it there, but he died many years ago, so any claim he had to the coveted stake has been automatically canceled.

Hank Sommers was the guy who put it there on a day late in October about 1903. The cache consisted of twelve sacks of rich ore from the old Neglected Mine on Monument Mountain. It was a sylvanite ore and among the richest that was ever mined in the fabulous mining district of southwestern Colorado. The ore was thoroughly impregnated with native gold, or it consisted of nuggets of the pure metal with specks of quarts adhering to it.

"There wuz nuggets of all sizes in that batch of highgrade," said Sommers in describing the lot, "all the way from the size of a pea to as big as a hen egg."

Sommers was a cook by trade, and for several weeks prior to the day he cached this ore, he had been employed in the boarding house at the Neglected Mine. On this particular day, however, he was on his way to Durango, a thriving mining and agricultural town located in the Animas valley at the foot of the mountains, and about twenty miles southeast of the Neglected Mine. Sommers had quit his job as cook the evening before and on this day was hiking to town.

The main trail from the mine to Durango wound around the mountain peaks from the mine to the Falls Creek divide a distance of about five miles. Here it climbed up and over a mountain called Cape Horn, a steep and rocky promonotory, but from this point it took a pretty direct course as it zigzagged its way down Barnes mountain to Durango. This trail was a busy thoroughfare at that time when mining at the Neglected was in its heyday. Several pack strings of burros traveled over it regularly in packing ore from the mine to the smelter in Durango, and in carrying supplies back to the mine. In addition to these pack trains there were people going back and forth between the mine and town.

Miners traveling on foot from the mine to Durango didn't follow this main trail, however. They would leave the trail somewhere along the divide at the head of Falls Creek and follow easterly down that watershed to the highway in the Animas valley, coming out on that thoroughfare eight or nine miles north of Durango. It was pretty easy to catch a ride along this main road on some farm wagon or buggy going to town.

This same route was the one followed by high-graders in transporting their purloined ore from the mine to town. The high-graders selected this rough and rugged route, not because of greater convenience but rather to avoid publicity and the suspicions that might be aroused because of a miner's transporting a heavy load on his way out from the mine.

Miners were ingenious in working out methods of getting the richest nuggets out of the mine and were clever in ways of transporting their contraband to "brokers," secret refineries, or other places where it could be converted into cash for themselves. High-grading made an excellent source of added revenue to any miner's income; and it was quite generally practiced in all mining circles. High-grading itself was not looked upon as a crime by mining people; it was the getting caught at it that was the misfortune. The attitude was: Wherever there is gold it is natural for men to try to get personal possession of it. In high-grading the miners were getting possession, illegally, of gold which the mine owners already possessed, and the owners were constantly trying to prevent successful efforts of the miners.

A rough sort of code of ethics had grown up around high-grading practices: A miner would never tell off on another one but would be quick to pass a tip if danger of detection threatened, and no man was supposed to bother another man's cache of high-grade, whether that cache was inside or outside the mine. This last rule was not always strictly adhered to and sometimes the repercussions for its violation were serious. If a man got caught molesting another's cache of highgrade he would get shot or seriously beaten up. It was less serious to get caught by legal authorities than it was to get caught high-grading from another high-grader. It was done to some extent, however, in spite of the risk, and when successful, it paid off mighty well. Under favorable circumstances a majority of men were tempted to try it. Some of them got away with it successfully but others never lived to tell the story.

Sommers knew these facts and conditions on that bright October morning as he coursed along through the timber and scattered, brushy undergrowth down the long mountain slope toward Falls Creek. He was not following any regular trail because none existed in this area. He was merely making his way to the trail along the creek. He regretted that his work as cook in the boarding house had afforded him no opportunity to add to his income by high-grading a little, as he knew that most of the miners had done. The pay check in his pocket would not be a very substantial winter's grubstake. He had to find some way of adding more to it.

And suddenly the opportunity of doing so presented itself! As Sommers was passing by a small clump of quaken aspen trees he noticed an unusual hummock in the grove, covered with leaves, and from one corner of this hummock protruded the end of a canvass ore sack—and that sack was full of ore! A high-grader's cache, and Sommers had accidently stumbled upon it! Here was a ready made opportunity, if there ever was such a thing!

Some high-grader on his way out had left his treasure at this isolated and hidden spot, while he had gone on to town to make arrangements to get his gold transported the rest of the way.

When Sommers had convinced himself that no one else was in the vicinity and that he was indeed alone and in no immediate danger of getting shot or having his head bashed in because of molesting the cache, he proceeded to make his investigation. Twelve sacks of high grade, gold nuggets and rich pieces of quartz, worth at least calculations $50 per pound, and every sack weighed about 60 pounds, $36,000 (at old price of gold) in one lump! To a wage-earner in 1903 this amount would be equal to a king's ransom. It would make him rich.

With Sommers the problem was not one of ethics, but of how to get away with it in order to avoid detection.

Obviously the first thing to do was to remove the treasure to another hiding place where the original owners would not find it. Sommers picked up one of the sacks and set out around the mountainside in quest of such a spot.

About 300 yards away he found a place that suited him. It was in a clump of spruce trees on a small bench of the hillside. Here the leafmold was deep and soft so he could dig a pit in it with his bare hands—the only implements he had. While digging a hole to cache the first sack in, it occurred to him that by emptying the contents of the sacks into the pit, and returning the empty sacks to the spot where he found them, he could more effectually promote the success of his own scheme. In the first place it would require less room in the trench for the loose contents of the sacks than it would for the individual sacks themselves, and the pit would be easier to cover effectively; and secondly, by returning the empty sacks to the original spot he would be eliminating any doubt in the minds of the other highgraders about the exact spot where they had made their cache when they returned and found the empty ore bags there.

When Sommers had completed his transfer job, he had a neat pile of empty ore sacks in the aspen grove where the full ones had been, and in a hand-made trench some 300 yards away he had more than 700 pounds of rich ore and nuggets—a tidy fortune that when converted into money would make him independently rich.

"I didn't put all that gold into the trench," Sommers told me later. "I took some of it with me. I couldn't carry much of it, but I did cram a few handfulls into my overalls pockets. I guess I had about three pounds of it with me. Later on I sold that ore to a broker, an Italian that had a saloon on Main Street in Durango a little way below the Strater Hotel. I got $100 for it, and o'course that broker figured on doubling his money on the deal."

Sommers took great care in covering over the trench in which he had hidden his fortune so that no tell-tale trace of it would show on the surface. He packed most of the leafmold back into it to cover his ore, and scattered the rest evenly around the spot; then he broke a small branch from one of the trees and painstakingly swept over the entire area to give the place a natural appearance. Of course he reasoned that he would not be fooled by this deceptive appearance when he came back in a few days to recover his treasure. He noted a peculiar shaped root from one of the trees that extended about 4 feet along the surface of the ground on the upper edge of the little bench. The cache was only a few feet below that root and lay parallel to it. That was an excellent natural marker, he thought.

Sommers didn't want to leave any artificial marks, such as tree blazes, to indicate the location of his cache, for fear such marks would attract the attention of other passersby and betray the secret place of his fortune. Although he had never been through this section of the country before, he felt sure he could return to this exact spot by instinct; but to help guide that instinct he took careful note of some natural landmarks. Off to his right he could see the white, sandstone bluff on the mountain side east of the Animas valley just above Durango, and farther up this same range of hills, and almost directly opposite from where he stood, he could see another promonitory. In the immediate vicinity he noted that just across the canyon, a dead tree, denuded of bark and branches, had fallen against a tall green spruce in such fashion as to form almost a perfect triangle and through the top of this tringle he could see a large rock in the bed of a gulch coursing down the hillside a short distance beyond the trees. This combination of natural objects made a definite and accurate marker, Sommers reasoned, that would have no significance to anyone else that might pass that way. And there would be no other spot where these objects would be in exactly that same relation. If, by any chance, he became confused about location of his cache when he returned to get it, all he had to do was to find the leaning tree, and from that, work out the point from which he could see the big rock through the tip of the triangle, and that point would be exactly on his cache.

Happy in the success of his venture so far, and confidently looking forward to a future of ease and independence which his golden treasure would provide for him, he resumed his journey to town. To eliminate any chance of meeting anyone who might be coming back up Falls Creek to get the highgrade, Sommers took out around the mountainside to the right, crossing ridges and canyons in the course of his travel in a wide circle to avoid the Falls Creek trail completely. He finally came down onto the highway in the Animas valley at the old Home Ranch about two miles below the juncture of the Falls Creek trail with the road. This route was rough traveling, but with two pockets full of gold pounding him on the legs with each step, and the pleasant thoughts of so much more safely hidden back up the mountain, Sommers did not mind the difficulties of the hike. He was happy, as only a man who has just struck it rich can be.

It was getting dusk when Sommers got into Durango that evening. The first place he headed for was the old Horseshoe saloon to get a drink of whiskey and to cash his pay check.

He had just swallowed his first drink and was pouring his refill when he heard a familiar voice call out: "Hi Hank, when did you get to town?" "Just got here," replied Hank as he turned to look at his interrogator, a miner by the name of Collier who with his partner, Schley, had quit working at the Neglected mine a few days before Sommers had. Collier and Schley had been employed in the mine for several months previously. They were excellent miners, and through long experience in mining, they were thoroughly schooled in all the tricks of the trade, including the precarious art of high-grading. That they had a tidy little stake in highgrade cache out somewhere when they left the mine, Sommers had no doubt, but where it was hidden he had no idea.

"How did you come down?"

"Walked," replied Sommers.

"Which way did you come?" asked Schley, apparently more to make conversation than for any other reason. When Sommers replied, "Falls Creek," he was startled to note that the partners gave each other a quick but furtive glance. Mindful of a pile of highgrade hidden back up on the mountain, and that these fellows had been working at the mine, although that highgrade might not be theirs, Sommers quickly amended his reply by saying:

"That is, I started down that way but got lost and finally wound up on the road down below the Home Ranch. Have a drink?"

They all had a drink. Sommers cashed his check. He was all nervous inside now and anxious to get away from these fellows lest they notice that he was ill-at-ease, but to leave them abruptly wasn't the thing to do. Miners, just arrived in a saloon, after several weeks spent in the mountains, didn't do that way. To do so would sure arouse suspicion of him, especially so if that highgrade belonged to these fellows.

And Sommers did not want either of these men, much less so both of them, either to suspicion him or to have a spite at him. Either one of them could be mighty tough and mighty cruel when provoked, and they were both powerful men physically. Sommers had seen a demonstration of their physical strength and of their cruelty in a fight they had had with a couple of other men at the mine shortly after he had begun working there. Collier and Schley had beaten those fellows up unmercifully and had seemed to enjoy doing it. Sommers did not want any such experience to be his; and he knew very well that if the highgrade he had found, and had hidden elsewhere, belonged to these men and that if they suspicioned him of having gotten it, they would give him a lot rougher treatment than they had given to the men at the mine. He figured they would beat him to death, and Sommers didn't want to die yet.

His inner tension eased a little, however, when Collier and Schley each bought a drink successively and the conversation veered away from his personal activities and switched to those of other employees at the mine. But Sommers still had his pockets full of highgrade and he was fearful that the unnatural hang of his overalls would be noticed by these men whose extensive experience had taught them all the telltale marks of the tricks of the trade. To avoid making any undue display of bulging front pockets, he kept his position of "belly up" to the bar, like a pregnant woman standing behind a waist-high piece of furniture to conceal her condition.

On the pretext that he needed a bath and to change his clothes, Sommers left Collier and Schley at the bar and walked out of the saloon. His first act when he got away from them was to go to his room and cache away the highgrade he had in his pockets, but he was careful to avoid the other two miners the rest of the evening. Cautious inquiries about them the next afternoon gave him the information that they had gone deer hunting that morning. Deer hunting, indeed, thought Sommers to himself. They are using that as a blind to go for the highgrade on Falls Creek.

He suspicioned this even more a couple of days later when Collier and Schley hunted him up purposely to make further inquiries about his trip down from the mine—which way he had come, had he seen anyone along the way or had he seen any fresh tracks, either of humans or animals anywhere along his route. Sommers had schooled himself for just such an encounter since he had met the two men in the saloon on his first night in town. He got through the conversation without revealing anything about the hidden ore, but these incidents caused him to change his plans.

When he had cached the ore, he had intended to return immediately with pack stock and bring it to town, but now he was afraid to do that. If that highgrade belonged to these men, and Sommers was now convinced that it did, they would be on the lookout for anyone cashing in that amount of highgrade; and woe would be to any man they suspicioned. Sommers did not want to be that man. The highgrade was safe, he reasoned, and could wait his convenience to get it. He would bide his time until these fellows went out on a job somewhere and then he could safely bring the ore to town. Instead, they stayed around town until a big storm, early in November, covered all the high country with a deep blanket of snow. Reluctantly Sommers gave up any plans he had about recovering his cache immediately. He was confident that he could return to the very spot where it was when the ground was bare, but he was not so sure he could with a covering of snow. It was better, all things considered, to wait until spring when all the snow had melted off.

Work was scarce around Durango that winter. Sommers lived on his limited savings and on his extensive hopes—hopes for a fortune when spring came and the snow went. Late in March he got a job in a logging camp over near Dolores, but he had to agree to stay on the job until July 1. This was a bit later than Sommers wanted to stay away from Falls Creek, but he reasoned it would work out all right and all the snow would surely be gone from Falls Creek by that date.

Schley died following an attack of pneumonia that winter, and early in the spring Collier left the country for a mining camp in California. These events left the coast clear for Sommers to recover his cache and convert it into cash. He was so impatient that he could hardly wait for July 1 to come.

It was after the big celebration of the Fourth, however, before he set out for Falls Creek and the golden hoard for which he had waited so many months. Since he was not familiar with the trails for livestock in that rugged locality. he decided to reconnoiter on foot first.

He had no misgivings whatsoever of his ability to find the location of his cache. He remembered the markings well. All he needed to do was to go up Falls Creek to some point near its source and then climb the brushy slope on the west side to a point from which he could see the white bluff and the other promonotory on the east side of the Animas valley, then find the exact spot by sighting through the apex of the triangle formed by the leaning tree to the big rock in the streambed opposite. It was all just as simple as that.

He was so sure of success and so eager to possess his fortune that, along with his lunch stuff, he carried an extra canvas sack in which he intended to carry back with him several pounds of the nuggets.

He was so eager to get up to his cache that he almost tired himself out climbing the long grade from the floor of the Animas valley to the beautiful mountain glen of Falls Creek above the cataract where that rivulet cascades over the high bluff into the Animas river.

Falls Creek valley did not look the same to him on this occasion as it had appeared in his view of it from the mountainside the previous autumn. It seemed smaller, narrower, and more shut in than it did then. It didn't seem like the same place, but he did not let this circumstance perturb him. He accounted for it from the fact that he was entering it from the opposite direction from which he had viewed it the year before. The landscape would come into proper perspective, he reasoned, when he had traveled far enough up the canyon to be in the immediate vicinity of the route he had followed the previous October.

Steadily he plodded on up the trail, all the while keeping a constant watch for some familiar landmark on some ridge or in some ravine that serrated the mountainside west of the creek. He saw none. Finally when he came on top of the divide between Falls Creek and Buck Canyon he realized he had gone past his goal, and was at least a mile too far north and east of his cache.

The whole country seemed different in appearance from what it had been the autumn before. Then it looked quite bare, more bold in outline and more expansive; now it seemed more "filled up," more softened by the verdant covering of undergrowth and forest in full leaf. Bare spots and minor landmarks blended inconspiciously with the sylvanian mantle. The altered natural condition somewhat confused Sommers.

He was not baffled for long, however. From his position on this high ridge he could see his two prominent landmarks on the opposite side of the Animas Valley. They were certain, unmistakable, and unchangeable guides that would lead him to his treasure.

All he had to do now, he reasoned, was to travel around the brushy, serrated mountainside west of him at about this same level so he could keep his landmarks in view and he would arrive right at the location of his cache. He was sure he would recognize the spot whenever he got to it, but any difficulty he might have in this regard would readily be dispelled by the leaning tree, the triangle it formed with the live one, and the rock to be seen through its apex. The whole thing just the same as in the bag.

In a short while now he would be scooping gold nuggets into the ore sack he had with him, and would be off on the back trail to town to convert them into money. How many pounds should he take? How many could he conveniently carry? No use to be a hog on this occasion because he would bring pack stock and get all of the ore in a few days. Ten pounds, he figured, would be about right for this time. That would not be a heavy load and could be converted into a nice little stake of $400 or $500; and he sure wanted to possess some of that gold for the sheer joy and satisfaction of it. It would be the most wonderful thrill of his life.

He crossed over on to the opposite mountainside, got his bearings on the two landmarks which he could see plainly from this point, and eagerly set out to find his cache. Using the white bluff and the high promonotory as guides for his course, he worked his way around the mountain to a point far south of the vicinity he had traveled through the year before, but yet he had not found any spot that looked familiar to him. This puzzled Sommers a little bit. How had he missed the place, and why hadn't he seen the more immediate landmarks adjacent to his cache?

He went back over the ground again, very carefully this time, but again failed to find any group of trees, either aspen or spruce, or any other object he could positively identify. He was completely puzzled by this time, and more than a little worried about his failure. He set out again on his quest, determined to define the limits of the area in which he could see the white bluff and the promonotory across the Animas Valley, and then to search thoroughly in that area for his more immediate landmarks—the leaning tree, the triangle, and the big rock. Much to his surprise and his chagrin he could see his chief landmarks from such a wide area and from so many different points that they ceased to be of any specific value to him as definite guides to any specific spot. They were excellent general landmarks to designate the general area, but he did not need any such designation as that. He knew the whole country and he knew this was the general location in which he had buried his gold. But it takes more than a general location for a man to find one specific small spot in several hundred acres of brush and timber land. It takes some specific surface markings to be able to do that. Sommers immediately began to hunt for his specific natural markings, but he could never find any of them that he could recognize—not even the clump of quaken aspen where he had first found the pile of sacked gold.

But he never gave up his hopes of finding his buried treasure.

Hope is the one thing that the treasure hunter never relinquishes. Each separate quest may end in failure but always hope springs anew that some trivial occurrence may happen to make the next trip a success and bring a golden reward to compensate for all past disappointments.

Until he died several years later, Sommers never gave up the hope that on some trip back into the Falls Creek country he would discover some telltale indication that would lead him to the rediscovery of his buried fortune. (I accompanied him on one of these expeditions, and although we did not find the gold, I had a grand outing.)

And that fortune has increased 75% in its value since Hank Sommers's time because of the greater price of gold in these later years; instead of $36,000 it would now be worth more than $60,000.

But what happened, what became of the natural markings that Sommers so carefully noted? Why couldn't he ever find them again?

To an experienced outdoorsman the answer to these questions are both simple and logical. Sommers made his cache late in the autumn when most of the leaves had fallen from the trees, and when all the seasonal vegetation, like grass and weeds, had matured and were no longer a ground covering. At such a time the landscape would look bare, and the whole country would stand out in bold outline.

When Sommers came back the following July, all the vegetation was in full leaf, and this condition changed the surface appearance of the district to such an extent that it made the country look "filled up" to him. This condition became a confusing element, and his faulty observation of specific details in nature made it impossible for him to recognize any specific spot or group of trees under the naturally altered conditions he found there the following July.

Heavy winter snows and the spring thaw and runoff were natural forces that destroyed his specific markings, or altered them beyond his recognition. The leaning tree that formed the hypotenuse of the triangle was dislodged by some winter storm and fell to the ground, perhaps breaking into several pieces in the process, and rolling down the mountain while the rock visible through the tip of the triangle was dislodged by some spring freshet and rolled down the stream bed some distance from its original position. The exposed root paralleling his cache, and almost covered over by an overhang of leafmold, perhaps became completely hidden by the overhang dropping down over the root. So as nature had made the marks Sommers used to locate his cache, she also erased those same marks to conceal his golden hoard, and there it remains to this day. But some day a fortunate traveler, possibly a deer hunter, passing by that spot may note a slight depression where the leafmold has settled along the trench in which Sommers buried his gold, and along the bottom of this depression the traveler will find small pieces of rich ore protruding that will be the "open sesame" to a buried treasure of $60,000 in virgin gold.

A Word About the Frontispiece Map

The San Juan region of Colorado is a big area. A much larger scaled map will be required to pinpoint treasure caches and lost mines. However, the general location is given on the large frontispiece map of the area and also on the sketch map in the first picture section of the book.

Treasure caches and mines are located by number, the wagon roads and toll roads by letter. One exception might be noted: the Spanish Trail along the Continental Divide is indicated by short arrowheads, the wagon roads by dots (. . .), which parallel modern-day roads on the map. An example of an earlier toll road is that of the road in the Animas Canyon at Silverton which became a railroad bed in 1881-2 when the Denver and Rio Grande R.R. was building up the canyon.

The Spanish Trail indicated was used as a high land (alternate) road for mule pack trains and bullion trains. Tree blazes which are very old have been located along the trail and bear evidence of being made by Spaniards rather than Indians or mountain men.

The map should be of value to the present-day historian who wishes to interpret the history of this region.

Guide to Frontispiece Map

Code	Name	Location			
A	Ophir Pass (toll road)	T 42 N,	R	9	W
B	Rico-Scotch Creek-Hermosa Park	T 39 N,	R	10	W
C	Durango-Thompson (toll)	T 35 N,	R	12	W
D	Silverton-Durango (toll)	T 4 N,	R	7	W
E	Durango-Pagosa	T 35 N,	R	9	W
F	Animas Forks-Lake City	T 42 N,	R	5	W
G	Stony Pass				
	Silverton-Del Norte	T 41 N,	R	6	W
H	Rainbow Route				
	Silverton-Ouray	T 41 N,	R	4	W
I	Pagosa-Del Norte	T 35 N,	R	41	W
J	Telluride-Dallas (Mears)	T 43 N,	R	9	W
K	Telluride-Ames via Sargents	T 42 N,	R	9	W
KX	Ames-Rico				
R	Spanish Trail (alternate)	T 39 N,	R	2	W
S	Tierra Amarillo	T 34 N,	R	1	W
T	Old Spanish Trail	T 32 N,	R	1	W
		to T 36 N,	R	12	W

Note: Reference is made to locations of lost mines, lost caches of bullion, or lost ores of silver and gold, and to toll roads and trails by townships.

The tables included make use of the government system of land measurement and locations of given areas in the United States in terms of the township.

The numbers increasing north (N) are township (T) numbers. The numbers increasing west (W) or east (E) are the Range (R) numbers.

The town of Silverton. Colorado near the upper left center of the map is located T 41 N, and R 7 W. The area covers 36 square miles.

Lost mines, etc. are located on the map by code, 1, 2, etc., tollroads and trails by letters such as A, B, etc.

Limitation of space makes it necessary to omit stories on items 11, 12, and 13.

Code	Name of Mine, or Cach.		Location		
1.	Lone Wolf Mine	Parrott Peak	T 36 N,	R 11 W
2.	Lost Clubfoot Mine	Parrott Peak	T 36 N,	R 11 W
3.	Venison Lode Mine	Parrott Peak	T 36 N,	R 11 W
4.	Enterprise Blanket (Mined out)	Rico	T 39 N,	R 11 W
5.	Cache (Stolen Highgrade)	Rico		
	Indian Ridge (Orphan Butte)		T 38 N,	R 11 W
6.	Lost Estes Mine	Silverton	T 39 N,	R 8 W
7.	Lost Carson Mine	Silverton	T 39 N,	R 8 W
8.	Baker Brother's Seam	Silverton	T 40 N,	R 8 W
9.	Golden Fortune (Cache)			
	Rio Grande River		T 40 N,	R 5 W
10.	$40,000 Dinner (Cache)			
	Rio Grande River		T 39 N,	R 5 W
11.	Mina Perdida La Ventana		T 39 N,	R 6 W
12.	Cache from Mina Perdida La Ventana		T 38 N,	R 2 W
13.	Search—actual hunt for Mina Perdida La Ventana and Cache			
14.	Stewart Placer Pagosa Side Continental Divide		T 39 N,	R 3 W
15.	Utes Dump Gold (Cache) Pagosa Chimney Rock		T 34 N,	R 4 W
16.	Talk and Share It Cache Gold (Arboles)		T 32 N,	R 5 W
17.	Hotter's Famous Rock Lost Rock of Gold Durango Area		T 37 N,	R 10 W
18.	Old Florida Mine Durango		T 38 N,	R 7 W
19.	Fall Creek Gold (Cache) Durango		T 37 N,	R 10 W